childrens KID
Blizzard 1880

THE

SOURCING

SOLUTION

THE

SOURCING

SOLUTION

A Step-by-Step Guide to
Creating a Successful Purchasing Program

Larry Paquette

ⵗAMACOM

American Management Association
New York • Atlanta • Brussels • Chicago • Mexico City • San Francisco
Shanghai • Tokyo • Toronto • Washington, D.C.

This publication is designed to provide accurate and authoritative
information in regard to the subject matter covered. It is sold with the
understanding that the publisher is not engaged in rendering legal,
accounting, or other professional service. If legal advice or other expert
assistance is required, the services of a competent professional person
should be sought.

Library of Congress Cataloging-in-Publication Data

Paquette, Larry.
    The sourcing solution : a step-by-step guide to creating a successful
purchasing program / Larry Paquette.—1st ed.
        p. cm.
    ISBN 0-8144-7191-9
    1. Purchasing. I. Title.

HF5437.P368   2004
658.7'2—dc22

                                                            2003019914

Printing number

10   9   8   7   6   5   4   3   2

To my wife, Pat Stearns, who believed in me
and provided encouragement
through all the years and midnight hours
spent in learning my craft. Thank you.

Contents

Acknowledgments

THANKS TO THE TUESDAYS—what surely must be the most successful writing group in the country. They exhibited patience and reader distance in critiquing the work as it was being created.

Special thanks to Bonnie Hearn Hill and Hazel Dixon-Cooper. One is a mentor and a wellspring of knowledge, a warm and compassionate teacher. The other exhibited a quiet, persistent confidence in me, even when the black clouds of writer's doubt filled my being. For these two special friends in writing, I am truly blessed.

Introduction

LIKE ALL BUSINESS FUNCTIONS, purchasing does not operate in a vacuum. Success is dependent upon well-trained, professional sourcing specialists who work in concert with other organizational functions to attain the company goals. It is also dependent upon understanding the future direction of the specific business, the business climate in general, and the strategic initiatives required to meet the organization's goals.

If you are currently in a buyer position, have desires to get into purchasing in the future, or have been there for a while and are looking for a promotion opportunity, you must gain an understanding of what the future could look like and learn how to successfully work in the new millennium. Those who take the time to learn will get ahead in the new economy. Old-school purchasing personnel, mired in a rut of past practices, need not apply.

Throughout this book I will share with you many ideas, concepts, and suggestions, in some cases using several examples, to help with your quest for success. We will discuss areas of vital importance to your future, including contracts, vendor agreements and relationships, and knowledge sharing and forecasting, in addition to the electronic and technology changes that swirl about us. The payoff will come as a result of your open mind, hard work, and study.

Historically, the road to triumph in purchasing has been a process of beginning at the bottom and, through on-the-job-training, or OJT, moving up the chain as your experience grows. Becoming a successful buyer is a learning and training exercise, not something that is instinctive or based upon a background in general education.

I will make a clear presentation on purchasing today and give you an idea of what to expect in the near future. I will also give you some hints on the thought processes required to help the new buyer succeed in meeting her goals.

Perhaps you've been in procurement for a few years, and you have just been promoted to buyer or senior buyer. You perceive the need for a broader view of the job and the techniques of the future, more than you might have been exposed to in your organization. You feel well versed in your skill sets, but you are not sure they are complete or the ones you need to succeed in the future. This book will help you develop your career path.

I am also writing to the executive of a company with annual sales of less than $100 million, a slice of the business population making up the largest percentage of all companies in the country. As an executive, you've watched former customers and competitors slowly whither away and close shop, or become part of the ongoing consolidations that seem the order of business today. You are passionate about your independence but realize your business will be affected over the next few years in ways you've never conceived of or experienced in the past. It is clear that one way to remain both independent and competitive is to have a sourcing strategy in place. Well, in this book I will help you identify areas to focus on.

As you read today's magazines, it's easy for you as a representative of a smaller company to come away feeling inadequate in the sourcing arena. For example, you can't imagine your company attracting much attention for your $10,000 annual purchase of flathead screws on a $1 million auction site. How about an e-commerce order for $250 worth of paper supplies? It's not going to happen.

This book will make specific suggestions and point out specific techniques to help make the smaller company successful in the twenty-first century. It is not burdened with tables of statistics (often outdated before the glue has dried on the binder), dry discourse on obscure theories, or pontifications on processes that were mildly successful in the last century.

Prosperous sourcing functions of tomorrow will find their own niches of supply and determine how to successfully exploit them. I will share some ideas on how to compete with the big boys and girls.

This book focuses on an overview approach toward the fascinating area of business sourcing. During the course of my years in the field, I have learned a great deal. I know what works, what doesn't work, and, most importantly, what no longer works. I have learned the darker lessons of common sense and logic—how they can lead the unsuspecting and unthinking into a blind canyon of inefficiency at best, significant losses at worst. You will learn from my mistakes and forays down promising paths that lead nowhere.

I have worked in the Far East when it was the world leader in manufacturing efficiency and quality. I worked with JIT, SMED, and Kan Ban when most U.S. companies couldn't spell them, never mind emulate or implement these processes. I have been instrumental in creating many successful partnerships in Japan, Taiwan, Hong Kong, and China, and I still enjoy the unique experiences inherent in doing business in that part of the world.

I will share the lessons learned on the international business arena and help you make your first forays into this sometimes intimidating, but always fascinating, segment of world sourcing.

My background includes stints in inventory control, stockroom management, production control, and master scheduling. My various titles have included words like materials, production, production control manager, director of materials, operations, purchasing, and sourcing manager, to name a few. I have worked in industries involving heavy equipment, computers (in California's Silicon Valley), vending equipment, construction equipment, and hobbies and crafts.

The direction of this book is tilted toward manufacturing. The lessons, however, pertain equally to the service and distribution industries, among others. Wherever materials and supplies must be ordered, scheduled, received, and sold, the lessons discussed in this book apply. I will have met my goals in writing this book if you go away with a sense of something learned and a handful of tools to help you succeed.

THE

SOURCING

SOLUTION

CHAPTER 1

In the Beginning

IN THE PAST, purchasing was not the independent, profit-and-loss center it has evolved into today. In order for items to be ordered, there was a cumbersome, routine process to follow. The first step in the process was to acquire three quotes, then a purchase order was issued, the documenting quantity was ordered, a desired delivery date was set, and the calculated price was agreed upon. Once the details were covered, a hard-copy document was generated. A copy would be mailed to the supplier, and other copies would be sent to receiving, the stockroom, accounting, and the clerk's file for follow up.

Purchasing was considered a "cost of doing business" item, instead of a contributor to the company's bottom line. The purchasing department was customarily stuck in the back offices and outfitted with castaway furniture, broken-down chairs, and old typewriters. In extreme cases, purchasing was a clerical function, usually run by an older supervisor who knew a lot about the company and product, but who was not considered star material or a candidate for one of the glamorous front-office jobs.

Purchasing departments lacked a widely accepted level of standard, professional ethics. Their staff members were often considered coddled and spoiled by other employees. Purchasing personnel were frequently spotted in the company of salesmen at expensive restaurants. They were never at a loss for regular lunch appointments, and they usually could be counted on to miraculously obtain hard-to-get tickets to theaters and popular sporting events. Holidays were especially gruesome, and Christmas past often saw a parade of spirits, gift certificates, and envelopes marching through the company lobby, guided by suppliers and vendors.

Simple Beginnings

I began my career as a part-time stockroom clerk for a Caterpillar Tractor dealer in New England. My duties consisted of unloading the delivery truck, putting stock away, pulling repair shop and customer orders, and, when all else was done, sweeping floors and cleaning restrooms.

The parts manager did all local purchasing, ordering only items unique to our location. The larger, regular supply orders were delivered based upon plans developed and placed at the main branch located in a different city. This was my first exposure to centralized purchasing.

I was always fascinated by how the trademark yellow parts arrived every week like clockwork, in the right quantity, and at just the right time. How did someone a hundred miles away know what we needed and when we needed it? I was even more fascinated to learn that our stock arrived from huge, multimillion-square-foot depots as far away as central Illinois. Now how did they do that? Of even more interest, who did it?

With the passage of a few years and a promotion or two along the way, I became the parts coordinator at the main office, where the miracle of planning and purchasing unfolded before my inquisitive eyes.

Standard practice was to have inventory tracked on a bank of Kardex cards. Each preprinted yellow card detailed an individual part number, description, type code, cost, and perhaps sell price. Its ledger was a litany of penciled history, carrying a running tally of receipts and issues, how many parts were ordered and when, and a minimum-maximum quantity used to trigger a replenishment order. There might even be a lot-size requirement for order placement.

The Kardex file in this particular company was gradually being replaced by an automated system, and it was maintained only for high-value, shop rework items, such as turbochargers and track rollers. But it only took a peek into the old storeroom to understand the history contained in the thousands of dusty card trays previously used to plan parts.

Sourcing Today

A leap forward to the twenty-first century showcases the evolution that has occurred in the purchasing function. In name alone, purchasing has gone through several iterations, and although still the nomenclature of choice for many companies, it has also been referred to as procurement, the contract department, and, in more recent times, sourcing.

There now exist formal degreed sourcing programs at several prestigious colleges and universities. Many of them have chaired professorships in all aspects of sourcing. Seminars are widely available, and professional associations abound, most notably the Institute of Supply Management (ISM), formerly known as the National Association of Purchasing Management (NAPM). Countless books have been written on the topics and specialties involved in purchasing, and dedicated trade magazines are readily available.

Professional-level ethics have become second nature, and the days of suppliers trying to influence the purchasing decision with a bottle of wine or pair of football tickets, if not gone, are waning fast. Today, the standard policy at reputable companies is no personal gifts, nothing having more than a minimal dollar value, and nothing without the supplier's advertising on it.

Ironically, both suppliers and buyers are relieved by this new business order.

The Future

Most organizations have put together specific goals to be accomplished by their sourcing departments, and the importance of the function is reflected in the organizational charts. Vice presidents of sourcing report directly to the chief executive's office, and they report on the same level as other key executive functions, such as marketing, sales, and finance.

What kind of numbers are we talking about? According to a recent article in *Purchasing*, companies such as Bell South, IBM, DuPont, and John Deere are setting cost reduction goals of 3.5 percent to 7 percent per year. For most of these companies, that equated to over $1 billion or more per company, per year.[1] The expectations are high, the numbers are huge, and the possibilities are exciting.

Managing this growth has not been easy, nor is there anything in the stars to indicate that it will not continue this way into the foreseeable future. So enough with strolling down memory lane. Let's start looking at some of the topics and areas that are of vital interest in today's challenging world of sourcing.

Note

1. Anne Millen Porter, "Spend a Little, Save a Lot," *Purchasing* (April 4, 2002), p. 23.

CHAPTER 2

What Is Sourcing?

PURCHASING DESCRIBES BOTH a department and its modus operandi within an organization. It is a term that describes both the department and its function. Depending upon the variances and company culture involved, purchasing typically controls from 45 percent to 100 percent of the procurement dollars of an organization.

Purchasing department responsibilities cover a variety of activities related to the goods and materials consumed by or used within an organization. Depending upon company structure, these activities might include determining suppliers, vendor certification, conducting location, site visits, and background checks. Purchasing is usually a significant player in locating and qualifying suppliers for required products. It normally takes the lead in price quotes and negotiations and will make strategic recommendations based on any one or combination of the above activities. Purchasing conducts final contract negotiations, fosters agreement, and oversees the approval process.

Having gone through and completed these laborious processes, department staff and buyers will periodically requote materials to ensure they are still getting the best deal for the company. Meanwhile, the department is held accountable for the administration of the contract, verifying each nuance, vague clause, and last detail. In the event a disagreement arises as to the performance by either party to the agreement, purchasing is usually the referee and leader of the consolidation and reconciliation team.

Whew. I'm tired just writing about it, especially knowing just how unproductive and nonvalue-added many of these activities truly are.

Unfortunately, in an erroneous concession to common sense, past experience, and misplaced logic, many of these practices continue to this very day.

Effectivity Killers

A case in point: I recently experienced the following directives in a large manufacturing company I was associated with.

"You must get me at least three quotes on every item," insisted the new general manager. He explained it was the only way we could ensure getting the best deal for the company. Purchasing would then pick and choose the individual best price for the hundreds of items required for a new product in the developmental stage. Common knowledge assumed this to be the most effective way to obtain the best price for the company.

Arguments and discussions to the contrary fell on the proverbial deaf ears. The general manager had always done it this way, knew that he was right, and in the past had insisted on this process at each company he had been associated with. Experience had reinforced his instinct that this procedure ensured the best possible price.

It was classical thinking with a logical assumption. It was driven by common sense, and it was completely wrong. The reality was that we were not ensuring the best total cost package to the company. I knew just the opposite would be the result: The company would actually spend more total dollars by following this approach. Using a technique I call the "ten-minute-more analysis," which I will explain in greater detail in Chapter 17, I would prove how wrong this old procedure was.

Some of the advantages we overlooked and lost using this directive included the benefit of efficiencies obtained by one supplier making like products, a larger raw material order, a single delivery point for that material, and, of course, one phone call to one supplier for a question or status update.

Instead, each supplier quoted each item as a single, stand-alone product. This directive told them they may only get part "one" and not "two" and "three," which might be related or similar parts.

For example, steel is sold by the hundredweight (CWT to be more precise). Tube and bar stock are sold by the foot. Although we were a large consumer of steel, we were not large enough to afford the inventory investment and cash flow required to buy direct from the mill. All deliveries came from steel service centers, commonly known as distributors or service centers.

By breaking up the quotes and subsequent orders among multiple suppliers, the service centers had to drive their delivery trucks to multiple locations, delivering the same kinds of raw materials, in smaller volumes, to two or more of our suppliers making similar parts. The extra trips, smaller volumes, and requisite paperwork were all reflected in the vendor's raw material costs and in the prices quoted to us.

In the case where multiple suppliers were making similar parts, the loss of efficiency should be obvious. Instead of having to make only one setup on a turning center, for example, two or more companies were making similar setups. Often the only difference in the parts was length or hole location. Machining centers were less efficient, labor was more expensive due to the additional changeovers required, and the additional costs were reflected in the price charged to the company.

Total cost could well have been significantly less. The piecemeal quote process excludes discovering and taking advantage of these benefits. The only parties guaranteed to receive the best prices by using this process were the vendors.

Just as like parts are more effectively run together, the increased quantity of like or similar raw material also contributes to a reduction in total cost. This type of analysis plays a key role in the job of today's sourcing specialist.

In the end, the general manager's commonsense, work-increasing, and inefficient directive focusing on multiple quotes created no value and cost the company money.

As a buyer, how often have you followed this path? As a manager, how often have you issued this kind of directive?

What's in a Name?

Sourcing is the departmental name that is slowly replacing purchasing in companies structured for twenty-first-century business. It more accurately reflects the strategies and goals of forward-thinking businesses that plan to succeed on a global basis, in a global economy. Sourcing is a strategic goal, not just a functional department.

What if, instead of writing and administrating order documents, the sourcing function put together a plan and strategy to make all the players successful? Not only would it be working to attain the best total cost for the company, it would be working with suppliers to ensure continued, ongoing success for them as well. If, as a sourcing specialist, and I like this title much better than "buyer," your efforts were directed on a daily basis to achieving such success, don't you think you'd end up a company hero in short order with an employee of the month parking space? The answer is: Of course you would.

Sourcing Today

Under this grand new plan, sourcing's role is to locate the one company out there that can provide needed product better than anyone else. Make no mistake—you may have to turn over a lot of rocks to feel certain about the best fit. But the best fit exists, and your job is to turn over those rocks.

When beginning the discovery process, the first order of business is to understand what you are looking for.

Price is easy. Although at times it is considered a significant indicator, in many cases just the opposite may be true. Many commodities, from semiconductors to chemicals to computers to office supplies, are priced within a fractional percentage of each other. In these cases, the sourcing specialist must look to other avenues to differentiate one supplier candidate from another, such as service levels, payment terms, and delivery schedules.

The consequences of the best price, from a poor supplier, are well known and obvious. If the quality is poor, necessitating constant rejects and returns to the vendor, or if production lines are regularly impacted by stock-outs due to nondelivery issues, your job security will not be especially high because of the great price you obtained.

Focusing on price alone is a potential pitfall of centralized sourcing done from some remote office on the other side of the city, state, or country. To be successful, centralized sourcing must also be held accountable for vendor quality and performance issues. Corporate buyers may be heroes to the company for their incredible abilities at getting low-cost items on long-term, no-cut contracts. At the consuming site, these nine-to-five heroes turn out to be something less when their vendor cannot perform. The downside is that, as the local buyer, you are the one held accountable, not the corporate seagull who appears to have flown over you, did what seagulls do best, and then flew away.

A true sourcing specialist must look well beyond price to determine the final supplier. You also need to learn what is required of your vendor to supply the product you desire, so that you can clearly understand the cost of the process, its components, and the lead times to accomplish product completion.

I would never expect to go into serious negotiations with a supplier without fully understanding its process, and without knowing, within a small percentage, its costs to manufacture. An important key to success in any vendor agreement is to know almost more about the vendor's needs than your own, and perhaps understand them as well, or better, than it does.

Let's assume that you have done your homework. You understand your supplier. You're confident about the supplier's ability to be the lowest total cost supplier to deal with, and you know that the supplier understands what you want. Now is the time for the contract, right?

Let's see.

Sourcing Agreements

A recent conversation by a supplier began this way: "We've got to have a contract in order to ensure that we can guarantee our relationship and supply to you." The speech continued with the tired platitudes about needing to lock the business in with its suppliers, guaranteeing against unforeseen price increases, and allocating capacity so that someone else couldn't sneak in ahead of us.

My end of the conversation was simple. In too many instances, organizations hide behind pieces of paper instead of working together to create a true alliance. The paper gets in the way of creating and maintaining an effective partnership. Instead of sitting down and working out the next success for both parties, it becomes too easy to point to a clause in a contract and question each other's commitment or performance. Instead of working it out, both parties waste effort

attempting to address real or perceived slights or areas of nonper-
formance.

Once again running contrary to common sense, when there is no
contract, there are more reasons to work together to solve a problem
or improve the business relationship. New opportunities crop up all
the time, as do new markets and technologies not dreamed of when
even the most well-meaning contracts were signed. Instead of being
limited by an ink-stained document, try to see the lack of a contract
as an opportunity to encourage further growth for one or both of the
players.

Make a pact to work together to continually improve quality, reduce inventories, provide innovative recommendations and ideas,
and work toward constantly reducing prices. As a customer, you will
achieve the benefits of these tasks and the assurances that your supplier is working in your best interests.

Your supplier will be comfortable, feeling that you are solidly in
its corner, will be there for the long term, and will not bolt to the
next solicitous phone call offering product at a cheaper price. With
time, your partner will get so far down the learning curve that competitors will never afford to be able to break into your market. This is
a negotiating win-win situation, if ever there was one.

Knowing Your Customer

The last point I'd like to make in this section is the important task of
understanding your customers. Do you know who your customers
really are? Do you know their needs? Are you doing your best to learn
their requirements so well that you will be able to anticipate their
needs almost before they come to realize they have them?

The most successful companies make customer satisfaction a top
priority for every employee. Within these organizations, each individual is charged with doing everything within their power to please the
end customer.

This is true on the higher level, but for most sourcing organizations, its primary customers are likely within the same building or
plant site. As a successful sourcing specialist, your job is to set in
place all the tools and measurements to ensure that manufacturing
receives the correct part, in the correct quantity, at the right time.

At the same time, you should work toward constantly reducing the inventory levels of items waiting to be consumed, whether floor stock or warehoused. This will satisfy another customer, the financial department that monitors expenses and cash flow.

While you are working with your internal customers, don't forget the marketing staff, which is on the lookout for new products and processes to sell, as well as the materials needed to make them. Sourcing personnel should be working with marketing almost from the moment of idea inception to ensure a smooth, orderly journey down the development path to the final release to manufacturing.

Another internal customer you need to keep in mind is the sales department. Historically, sales has been trained to forecast its needs on the high side, thereby assuring a constant supply of product. Convince the sales department that you are focused on ensuring that the right product will be there when the external customer calls and places his order.

Summary

This is a very short introduction to sourcing and some of the tasks it includes. Many of these tasks are in new areas. In the past they were not considered a part of the purchasing function, but in today's brave, new, global world, they are. Today sourcing is considered a vital tool that contributes to an organization's future success.

I've given you a few things to look for in the sourcing process, and I will discuss more specifics as we move forward through the remaining chapters.

Low-Hanging Fruit

Income distributions

IN CHAPTER 8, I talk about Pareto's law, commonly known as the 80:20 rule. Pareto's law has been interpreted as saying that the largest return comes from the least effort, which certainly applies to sourcing. In any endeavor you undertake, the best opportunities are usually the easiest to identify and attain a significant result, what I refer to as low-hanging fruit.

The Internal Consultant

A significant portion of my career has been spent in visiting various company operations, having been tasked with a specific problem to solve. My first experience was at Ampex Corporation, a large audio-video broadcast equipment manufacturer during the early 1980s. At the time, the company was comprised of five divisions, with four major sites in the United States and other factories located in Europe and the Far East.

My first function was to manage foreign procurement for all the divisions. Once that department was organized and running well, I became a corporate-wide, manufacturing department problem solver. Officially titled corporate materials manager, I visited and spent time

13

in the company's many facilities. My role was to identify manufacturing problems and recommend solutions.

It was a delicate road to travel, because, although I was on site to investigate and solve problems, I reported to corporate headquarters. This functional dual role often led people to suspect me of being a corporate seagull, in other words, someone who had a reputation for flying over and leaving unpleasant droppings everywhere he went. Success came by convincing others that I truly was there to help, and by persuading them that success would be measured by their improving numbers, not tales brought back to headquarters in California.

In the years I worked in this position, I learned the importance of understanding my customer and the role that I could play in helping him to improve his operation. I learned that initial appearance was more significant than fact, and that working with people was more important than being right. From a sourcing standpoint, several valuable lessons were learned that remain applicable to this day:

❑ Identifying the low-hanging fruit is a matter of keeping your eyes and mind open.

❑ The opportunity often is not what management thinks it is.

❑ The solution is usually not the first idea that surfaces.

❑ If given a choice between a complex implementation and a simple idea, go with the latter every time.

❑ A quick, small success is more important than a long, drawn-out, larger one.

Opportunities for Cost Reduction

Opportunities for cost reductions and efficiency improvements exist everywhere, and a good sourcing specialist believes in walking around his facility, keeping his eyes and ears open for an advantage. Advantages exist everywhere.

One stop along the way will be the raw material warehouses. Look for stacks of goods from the same vendor or a limited number of vendors. How many days, weeks, or even months' worth of investment might this represent? Are great prices being obtained because your company is willing to purchase large lots in bulk, and then carry the material for an extended period of time?

Significant warehouse inventory levels can mean your company has become an unwitting ally in your supplier's business dealings. Your vendor may be passing through large delivery lots of product to you, while obtaining aggressive, high-volume prices from its supplier. Don't be a large-lot, long-term warehouse for your supplier.

Investigate whether the raw material might be converted to consigned inventory. In this case you might be willing to store the goods for the supplier, but not actually take title and create the financial liability until such time as you actually pull stock for consumption on the production line.

In this example, your vendor will continue to get volume purchase prices from its supplier, and you will continue to obtain a lower price. Both companies are sharing the scheduling risk to an extent; the change is that you are now sharing in the cost benefits.

Take the same walk along the production lines. Are there stacks of materials stored here? Are there excess parts and materials from jobs no longer running, or ones already completed?

You should feel two concerns in this situation. The first is that extra or old items likely indicate inventory or bill-of-material (BOM) record accuracy problems. These will play havoc with your longer-term purchasing and vendor inventory goals.

The second concern is finding staged inventory for work not scheduled until some time in the future. If the production line is staged in this manner, there are several risks, including loss of parts, obsolescence, damage, and movement without documentation. The result is poor inventory record accuracy and additional product costs.

Next, walk through the receiving department and finished goods warehouse. Check out extra storage in open areas between buildings and other obvious locations. Look carefully into these opportunities of converting excessive stored goods into cash.

In order to better understand opportunities for cost reduction, an action item for every person in procurement should be to learn to work closely with the cost accounting personnel in your facility. Take them to lunch, camp on their office doorstep, set up regular training meetings, but work with them to learn how material is costed, the cost to carry materials, the cost of capital employed calculation, and what a good number might be to use for simple analysis purposes.

Remember that every bit of stacked inventory, piled in warehouses, bulk, or on the production line, is cash lying idle, a wasted investment opportunity. Every dollar sitting in inventory is a dollar not available for future growth, improved efficiency, salary increases, or hiring of additional staff. In walking around your facility, learn that you are not looking at cartons, hardware, bottles, steel, or copy paper. You are looking at lazy dollars not working as hard as you do.

Step Not Blindly into the Night

In 2003, the cost of borrowing was low. My company at the time used a 29 percent rate of overhead to cover the cost of capital. This included the cost of renting money (interest rate), the risk of obsolescence, warehousing, damage and theft, insurance, and overhead, among others. Every $1,000 in inventory cost an additional $290 per year to sit there. The cost of the capital and the length of time it sat in the warehouses increased the total investment in idle parts. When taken as a total cost of procurement, lowered bulk purchase prices aren't quite as attractive as initially believed.

A funny, yet sad, story illustrates how misunderstood costs can be, and why it is so important that a good sourcing specialist understands and is able to work with the accounting numbers. This case illustrates why purchase price alone is not a measure of success.

In the mid-1980s, interest rates were climbing to the high teen levels, and borrowing costs were going through the roof. The cost of capital was likely in the neighborhood of 75 percent. Customers were extending out their payments to 120 days, and productivity was down. Some commentators at the time felt the country was in the throes of stagflation where growth was minimal, but prices continued spiraling up.

The case at hand was paper. This occurred at the corporate headquarters of the audio-video company mentioned earlier. There were a thousand employees scattered across a campus covering several streets, and the company consumed a lot of copy paper.

The corporate procurement function took notice, and, as part of its efforts to substantiate its worth to the company, started looking into the situation for cost-saving opportunities. The responsible buyer worked with all department heads, analyzed purchases over the previous three years, and verified that the company had been doing a lot of business with three major office supply companies.

The buyer consolidated the data, put the results out for bid to several new suppliers, and obtained several proposals in return. One featured an apparently interesting price reduction.

The quoted purchase price was lower than any level the company had ever paid in the past, and, in conjunction with its annual buy quantities, looked to contribute a significant savings to the company. All agreed it was a fine plan, and the contract was signed.

What was overlooked in the pell-mell rush to take credit for the cost savings was the price associated with the lowered cost. The evidence lay in the number of trailers and hundreds of pallets of paper that appeared at our receiving dock over the following weeks. Delivery volumes were out of line with usage rates. The immediate question to the receiving and warehousing supervisors was: Where were they going to be able to store all this low-cost paper?

In the end, the significant purchase price reduction actually cost the company more money, including warehouse and cost of capital, than before the agreement had been signed. The intent was good; the failure was in focusing on the pennies while ignoring the dollars flying away in cost of capital and lost overhead costs. In focusing on the purchase price, the buyer had overlooked the total cost of the deal.

The subsequent low-hanging fruit in this case was obvious. It was what to do with the hundreds of pallets of copy paper you couldn't help but trip over walking from one end of the campus to the other.

Why Cost Reductions?

A logical question at this time might be: Why put all the emphasis on cost reductions? When companies receive favorable press, it usually has to do with increases in sales, new products, a buyout, or a new alliance. It is rare to see much of anything in the general business press regarding cost reduction activities or achievements. Why then, do cost reductions garner so much attention in the sourcing world?

One way to measure cost reductions is to compare them to equivalent sales. Every company needs sales volumes to remain in business, and all companies look to future growth in this area as a yardstick of their performance and long-term potential.

However, no sales dollar is pure profit. After deducting expenses associated with producing the sale, such as inventory, labor, taxes, building expenses, and the light bill, there remain only a few cents for net profit. The earnings before income taxes (EBIT) is a quick gauge of the actual percentage of every sales dollar that makes it all the way down to the bottom line. If the EBIT is 10 percent, then ten cents of every sales dollar is making it through to the bottom line.

In equivalent sales at 10 percent EBIT, every dollar saved in the sourcing process, whether in cost reduction or efficiency, is equal to ten dollars in sales, when measured by net dollars flowing to the bottom line.

Opportunities Are Everywhere

Don't be afraid of looking for opportunities within your company, even if they are not directly related to a primary material cost reduction. Costs are insidious and have a tendency to grow in benign ways, and, once established, become difficult to eradicate.

Electronic commerce is a growing issue in the twenty-first century, and it is an area that this book addresses in many different forms. But even electronic support systems can be a contributor to costs, through difficult data maintenance requirements put upon the company and its personnel. When used effectively, it will be a significant tool for cost reductions.

One example is purchase orders. Purchase orders are created and maintained in some form of EDP system in most companies. Demands and forecasts are processed through a material requirements planning (MRP) system, the output is usually reviewed and scheduled by buyers or planners, and a final purchase order is placed. The systematic order shows the vendor, the dates placed and due, the scheduled deliveries, the product and quantity ordered, the price paid, the terms, and the means of delivery. All orders are easily available for study and review by the execution of a few simple keystrokes.

This being the case, why do companies maintain countless file cabinets stuffed with paper copies of old purchase orders? Why invest money in cabinets, the labor to sort and file away these orders, and the required floor space to keep them on hand? Why so much expense to duplicate existing information?

By eliminating this effort, a savings opportunity is created. And although it might not flow directly to a material cost savings of the kind sourcing departments are usually looking for, nevertheless it is still a number that contributes to improving the bottom line of the company's financial statements.

Another area of indirect cost savings to pursue is internal procedures that are inefficient and cost contributors. In a modern, electronic data-processing environment, which includes most companies today, there are countless tools to make the processing of business requirements more efficient and smooth. The way to avail oneself of these efficiencies often only requires a few more minutes of thought and analysis to determine a way to do it correctly.

Therefore, when confronted with processes that recommend manual tracking forms, action sheets, or status reports, turn into a stubborn mule of resistance, dig in your heels, and put on your most disgusted frown. The computer was designed to do repetitive tasks easily and much more efficiently than its human controller; figure out a way to let it accomplish the task, freeing the human for more effective use of her greater analytical and logical problem-solving skills.

More on Low-Hanging Fruit

By design, this chapter touches upon several topics and examples of low-hanging fruit. The message should be clear that, within most organizations, there are a number of opportunities to improve efficiency and lower the total cost of doing business. Sourcing is a prime mover in this area.

When searching out wasted cash investment in an organization, there are two other common opportunities

Safety Stock

This is a classic, expensive, and widely misunderstood bank account paying no interest and yielding no return on the company investment. Supposedly kept for short-term variations in scheduling, or worse, inventory accuracy fluctuations, in reality it is a number not routinely monitored for timeliness or accuracy. If the total investment of safety stock dollars were to be tallied in a company, the number would be staggering in most cases.

Instead of just-in-case inventory, spend the dollars more wisely by solving the root cause requiring the investment in the first place.

Data Accuracy

Very few companies completely understand the need for data accuracy on the factory floor, and more importantly, the price paid for not having it.

chain of probabilities

To illustrate, a typical factory might process incoming inventory through a receiving location, deliver it to the stockroom for storage, pull it to a work center, produce the goods, transact the work-order completion, deliver to a finished goods warehouse, and ship it to a customer. Seven functions, or gates, exist in this example. A factory claiming 95 percent data accuracy with this process actually has only a 66 percent chance of being correct, end-to-end (95 percent[7]). Even if the number is 98 percent, the actual throughput accuracy is still only 85 percent. Put another way, somewhere between 15 percent and 34 percent of the activities in this operation are wrong. Aren't you glad that your paycheck isn't processed with this level of accuracy?

Consider also that if the inventory records report one hundred items in inventory, and when you check there are only ninety-eight, your inventory record accuracy is not 98 percent, it is zero.

Each of these errors costs money in the form of lost inventory, expedite charges, or inefficiencies associated with a start/stop process.

Summary

It would be easy to demonstrate many other examples of cost reduction and efficiency improvement opportunities within the typical organization, each one low-hanging fruit ripe for the harvesting. The defining moment comes in identifying and getting your arms around them. Most require more attention and commitment to resolve than actual effort and hard work. Many can be addressed and eliminated by a simple process change.

The point is to keep your eyes open for opportunities, in whatever form they may present themselves. This is good sourcing, good employee behavior, and, in the end, an important contributor to long-term business success.

CHAPTER 4

Managing Your Vendors

IN THE NOT-SO-DISTANT PAST, placing orders was a more structured process. Once the material-planning group determined the needs, the requirements were forwarded to purchasing for placement. A preferred supplier list noted the recommended vendor and one or two alternates. A call was placed to verify price and delivery, and if everything came close to the requirements, an order number would be issued. The original copy of the purchase order was put in the mail, copies were sent to the accounting and receiving departments, the buyer filed his copy, and the job was done.

Good management practice dictated that every buyer requote her parts at least once a year, preferably every six months. It was also the buyer's responsibility to have at least two qualified suppliers for each item, and having three or more was worth a purchasing merit badge.

In the normal course of business, it was assumed that the total requirements pie be split at least 80:20 between the top two vendors. In this manner each supplier was a part of the team, and in the event that the major vendor went down for any reason, the second supplier would already be on line, qualified, and ready to take up the slack.

Flawed Decisions Result from Flawed Logic

I had an uneasy feeling about the assumptions behind this way of placing orders almost from the moment, early in my career as a junior buyer, when I was directed to follow it. Instinctively it felt misguided, even before I could reasonably quantify my reasons. After a few years of practice, I realized why this was so.

In the training classes that I occasionally host, I have a favorite saying that I still use to this day, and it is one you will run across in other chapters of this book. The reason it is still valid, even in the twenty-first century, is that old habits and thought processes, like the dragons in fairy tales, are difficult to slay.

"Every company should have at least two qualified suppliers for any given part number. Four would be better, and eight's great." This little exercise in exaggeration and absurdity illustrates my point.

Common sense and logic, if not judiciously applied, routinely contribute to poor decisions that can lead you down the path of business disruption. Requiring multiple sources is a classic example of one of those common-sense rules that is so logical that everyone knows it to be true.

I became a convert to the newly evolving procurement processes early in my career. I had experienced the vaunted Japanese manufacturing techniques in the 1970s, and I readily saw that they were on to something. I observed factories that were devoid of raw material inventory at the beginning of the day. These factories ran their normal production shifts, built their allotted product, and at the end of the day had no inventory left on the floor.

A company where the production floor holds no inventory or partially completed product at the end of the day has, consequently, no risk of damage, obsolescence, loss, or wasted investment.

I witnessed vendors who delivered product inside of a fifteen-minute window. Many of them repeated this process over the course of a day. Drivers backed their trucks into a designated receiving bay, and they unloaded cargo with modern material handling equipment designed to move pallets and boxes very efficiently. Without so much as a moment's delay or diversion, they delivered the material to the designated Kan Ban square directly at the point on the factory floor where it would be consumed. This was Just-In-Time (JIT) in action.

Make the Plan, Work the Plan

Production at these Japanese plants followed a plan that was developed and agreed to by all critical functions, including manufacturing, sales, production planning, and purchasing. Once the marching orders were finalized, the plan could not be changed. One executive I met at the time compared Japanese and American manufacturing methods this way: The Japanese make the plan and work the plan. Americans make the plan and change the plan.

Class "A" factories planned their material needs and scheduled product using a basic Kardex system. There was no need for a heavy investment in manufacturing or for purchasing data-processing equipment; both were perceived as an investment that added no value.

The Japanese were on to something. The design and technological capabilities of the factories rivaled the best that the United States had to offer. The Far East mentality was to invest in those tools and equipment that directly affected and improved the efficiency of the production line. If a computer could be used to design a more effective machine tool, to improve the interchangeability of required tooling, to speed up the manufacturing line, or contribute to improved quality and reduced defects, there was no question about making the investment.

Requiring sophisticated computers to plan material requirements, which could be handled effectively by a stable plan, the Kardex system, and attentive clerks, was viewed as a waste of valuable resources and a diversion from the task of constant improvements in efficiency.

More Flawed Logic

In the United States we were committed to taking a different approach. Perceived fact dictates that we procure required material from at least two sources.

To survive a calamity, such as the possibility of the primary supplier succumbing to a devastating fire, you must have a second source, ready to pick up the slack.

The apparent logic here fails under the scrutiny of analytical thought. The first anomaly is that you are paying more for the item by procuring it from two sources. The 80 percent supplier is not giving you the best possible price because you are not buying the highest volume possible. It knows you have another supplier on board for the balance of the business. The second supplier is only getting 20 percent of the business, so it is only giving you column pricing, most likely significantly higher than your main vendor.

The next point is that neither supplier is committed to you as a partner, and they are not as likely to come to your aid in a crisis. No matter how well it does, the top supplier realizes it can never get all of your business. The second supplier knows it is only second best and has no motivation to improve service.

The most fallacious argument for having a second vendor on line is in case the main vendor has a catastrophic failure. Assume that something like a fire, flood, or earthquake wipes out your key supplier. How likely is it that the smaller company will suddenly be able to ramp up to five times its present capacity of your product? Reality dictates that it can't, and thus you've been paying a premium price for an insurance policy that really won't cover you in the event of a catastrophe.

The wisest course to take, and one that most leading-edge industries are following today, is to find the best qualified supplier that you can, give it all your business for the products and processes it does best, and create a solid partnership allowing both of you to succeed and grow. In other words, put all your eggs in one basket, and then closely cultivate those eggs and watch that basket.

When a problem arises, note the level of responsiveness to your needs. Whether you need a short-term OSWO (Oh Shucks, We're Out), a critical redesign, or an effort to reduce cost, your partner, in knowing that you completely rely on him, will be more receptive to being first in line to help solve your problem.

More benefits of a singular relationship will become apparent in later chapters on negotiations and total cost of acquisition.

Keeping Your Eyes Open

Keeping your eye on the basket is also important. You, as a successful buyer, must build up a trustful relationship with your supplier, and you must have confidence in his ability to deliver on his commitments.

But being a prudent sourcing expert, it is important that you keep your pulse on the world of supply. You need to know exactly what is going on in your commodities and products regarding pricing, availability, raw materials, technology, and other critical changes.

In the late 1990s I was in charge of the steel procurement for a heavy equipment manufacturer with sales of approximately $200 million. We annually purchased in excess of 20 million pounds of hot-rolled steel, including tube, bar, sheet stock, and flame-cuts. The largest single component of this procurement was sheet stock, ranging from gauge size up to quarter-inch-thick plate.

We were procuring the steel based on a two-year contract that I inherited. Over the course of the last year of the agreement, I held regular meetings with the supplier of choice, indicating that I thought the price we were paying was significantly higher than market. I continually requested that the vendor look into this.

As I have already indicated, a first order of business for a sourcing specialist is to know his commodity, sources, and markets. In that vein, here's why I could make that statement with complete confidence.

I knew that the steel mills were delivering this product for eleven dollars per CWT (hundredweight), at the railhead at their plant. Transportation by rail was four dollars per CWT, delivered to the nearest rail yard. Delivery would be about two dollars, and fair markup was three to four dollars. Therefore, my price should never be more than twenty to twenty-one dollars per CWT, or twenty to twenty-one cents per pound. They were charging us upwards of twenty-three to twenty-six cents per pound, the agreement price. We were paying a 10 percent to 30 percent premium to market price.

How did I know that? Periodically I called in the steel manufacturers to discuss our needs and to inquire about mill-direct purchasing. I learned about prices, terms and conditions, the risks and savings of rail versus truck shipment, and the nuances of steel mill scheduling. From this I could calculate the additional inventory investment required, capital impact, total cost of direct purchase, possible impacts to our customers, and potential cost savings/expense. I knew my supplier's cost of product within a fractional cent.

When contract renewal time came up, we took a very hard look at this supplier's overall performance and commitment to us as a partner. After a round of competitive bidding, we decided it was in our long-term best interest to go with another steel vendor.

Had the original supplier been dishonest? No. Had he not honored his contract commitments? No, again. Where he failed was in not understanding that his customer was knowledgeable about the product, market, and availability. In other words, the customer had done his homework prior to contract renewal time. In the end, the supplier naively walked into the renewal negotiations expecting to walk out with a rubber-stamped contract renewal in hand.

The supplier committed the cardinal sin of taking her customer for granted. We took the proper action of knowing our product, requirements, markets, and supplier opportunities.

Future Think

Another way to manage your vendors is by setting very clear, detailed, and explicit expectations for his contributions for new products and ongoing process improvements.

The thought process is simple. Any given supplier does what it does all day, every day. If the supplier is as good as it should be to warrant your commitment as a partner, it possesses a wellspring of product knowledge earned over a lifetime of being in business. No matter how in-tune your company might believe itself to be, it cannot know everything there is to know about the product, certainly not as much as the supplier.

Take advantage of that experience. Train your vendors in what you do and how you use their products. Show them your process and production lines, share your concerns and issues, and ask for help in improving your efficiency and reducing costs.

Meet with key vendors regularly, and expect them to be armed with ideas and suggestions. If it makes sense, request that they attend new product and design meetings. Encourage them to contribute knowledge right from the beginning. In this way you can assume that many unexpected pitfalls will be avoided, while ensuring the most efficient, cost-effective design is used.

A good supplier will be able to suggest product consolidations to achieve improved economies of scale. It will advise which new technological advances in its market and product base might make sense for your company.

Summary

In a world of global customers and supply, it is imperative that the sourcing specialist of today has the drive and the ability to think creatively in developing relationships. She must be willing to entertain new concepts and ideas from suppliers she may not have been comfortable dealing with in the past.

The sourcing specialist should also be willing to study all aspects of her current vendor base, and look forward to their meeting the future goals and needs of the company several years hence. Those vendors that she determines are able to measure up to her company's needs must be trained in the new expectations of her organization, and in the difference in meaning between a simple, order-taking supplier and a true partner.

Today's sourcing specialist will need to think creatively about how to consolidate a great number of items under fewer vendor umbrellas. She must be able to run the numbers to understand the financials behind her recommendations and decisions.

The philosophical approach to managing vendors will also change. A partnership is different than a buy/sell purchase agreement, and, in order to be effectively exploited, the difference must be understood. New processes include the need to manage vendors by setting clear expectations for knowledge sharing, constant process improvements to reduce cost and improve efficiency, and recommendations on new products and technology. Make it clear that this is a partnership relationship. Make it clear that, as in a marriage, you will not bail out at the first opportunity, but also like a marriage, you expect a mutual commitment.

CHAPTER 5

Vendor Consolidation

IN THE NEW ORDER of sourcing activity, there is a definite emphasis on partnerships and vendor relations. Reducing the total number of suppliers is a worthwhile pursuit that fits under this same umbrella. There is a conspicuous movement away from past practices of having multiple vendors supplying a given part, product, or commodity. Today's companies are putting processes in place that rely upon a selected few partners to cover a broader range of their needs.

The Globalization of Customers and Resources

Globalization of the supplier and customer bases is a cornerstone in the business world today. Trade opportunities are no longer limited to around the state or around the country. They exist around the world.

If a company intends to be a successful player in the worldwide arena of commerce, it needs to anticipate and plan for two things. The first is the consolidation of business. Companies today are actively combining resources through outright purchase or absorption of previously separated companies, or by putting strategic partnerships together to pursue larger opportunities that would overwhelm a smaller operation. Such company growth in a market will create a business presence that can be difficult or impossible to overcome by a slower competitor.

The second activity that companies must anticipate is the consideration of the world as a resource. Although always a desirable goal, the previous practices of limiting sources to those readily known, easily investigated, or conveniently located are gone. Where fear of the unknown might have prevented the active pursuit of suppliers from new markets, emerging economic forces are taking that decision off the table. Business survival demands changes in our thinking regarding sources of supply.

Today's companies are sourcing raw materials from South America, subassemblies from Far East countries such as China and Vietnam, software and design from India, precision parts from Europe, and final assembly from Malaysia or Mexico.

It is a mandate for the contemporary sourcing department to seek out and discover effective resources, evaluate each for its total cost-effectiveness, and create key strategic alliances to ensure a constant flow of the goods and services desired.

Future sourcing opportunities are not limited to mining veins of new suppliers and vendors. The possibilities for cost-creep in business are many. Each, in turn, is also an opportunity to manage and take costs out of the process.

One example of a newly emerging cost-reduction opportunity is for shipping companies to begin breaking down containers in transit, resorting and repacking products into consolidated containers ready to ship to a destination city. Upon disembarkment, the containers are loaded onto a truck or railcar and whisked on their way. This can shave precious days, or even weeks, off product lead time.

Pushed further upstream, suppliers thousands of miles away are individually marking boxes with customer identifiers, shipping information, and documentation. This is in preparation for the container being broken down at a remote site, where individual shipments will be sent on their way directly to end customers, eliminating the importer's having to handle or transship product.

In order to be successful in this new market order, a company must be able to recognize and explore opportunities, no matter where they might appear. One contributor to this success will be the discovery of new processes, suppliers, and products, some with approaches you may have never before considered. Another obvious change is vendor consolidation.

Vendor Consolidation

Material Requirements Planning (MRP) was the first automated planning system to schedule raw material to support a factory-build plan.

MRP II (Manufacturing Resource Planning) was the natural evolution to vertically integrate other departments into the planning system. This included finance for sales and cash-required planning, the factory for labor loading and capacity planning, and sales for product availability planning.

The most current evolutionary product is referred to as Enterprise Resource Planning (ERP), which takes MRP II to the next level for tying point-of-sales data directly into the forecasting model.

MRP, MRP II, and ERP are effective tools in planning the individual items typically required to build a final product. The outputs can be sorted by vendor, part number, commodity class, or any of a dozen different ways useful to sourcing personnel.

When undertaking vendor consolidation, the place to begin is the MRP run. In studying the typical output, it should become obvious that a significant number of similar items are supplied by a number of different vendors. Your study should confirm that each vendor has different lead times for product, different lot sizes for delivery and price breaks, different quantities per package size, and pricing models all over the universe. It will not take long for the modern sourcing specialist to spot the opportunity.

As currently structured, each of these items now requires buyers to create and release new purchase orders, or reschedule and resize existing ones, covering a number of vendors. The obvious question is: Why are you doing this?

In the past, the first recommended solution that many companies came up with when faced with this situation was a form of manual ordering system, usually Kan Ban. This made sense for repetitive orders for simple products, such as hardware or packaging. (For more on Kan Ban, see Chapter 11.)

Under this system, a card is sent to purchasing to release a new order once a certain bin or pallet is opened or delivered to the production floor. The planning assumption is that the lot size on the Kan Ban card covered the vendor's delivery lead time, and was a proper size for production requirements.

But when had the Kan Ban cards last been reviewed? Was the supplier information, prices, lot size, even the floor location, current and correct? Have seasonal effects been accounted for? Were there changes in the number of operating shifts?

Where Are the Kan Ban Cards?

Downtime is universally expensive, and, when caused by unplanned material shortages, will garner the highest level of attention by the factory management team. Under these circumstances, this is not the kind of spotlight a sourcing specialist normally enjoys.

I was involved with one situation where critical shortages were occurring with an ever-increasing frequency. Weekly shortage meetings became daily, hot lists proliferated, and priorities changed almost hourly. Something was inherently wrong in the process.

I looked at a few examples of these shortages and drilled down to the underlying issue, which often could be laid at the feet of an inaccurate or lost Kan Ban card.

Whether through lack of attention, inadequate training, low expectations, changing priorities, or misunderstanding, it was obvious that we were doing a poor job of managing the Kan Ban process. We could easily do a top-down review of our process and reimplement what was not currently working, but was this the smart thing to do?

Let's Try Something New

What would happen, I reasoned, if we approached those current suppliers whom we felt were willing to work with us, and explained our situation to them? We could pick our top two or three product classes that were causing us the most difficulty, make available all pertinent information, and encourage our potential partners to go away and study the situation. My expectation was that they would return with one or more creative solutions.

After careful consideration, I implemented the plan. Step one was to gather the affected part numbers and specification sheets, along with the best-estimated annual requirements. We considered the name of the current supplier and the price paid as confidential information, not to be shared.

The second step was to clearly identify our expected response from the bidders, and the criteria upon which we would base our decisions.

We asked each bidder to take the package away, give it careful study, and come back with its best overall proposal. The total cost of acquisition would be the decision-making criteria, not just best possible price. Preference points would be given to suppliers that bid on the complete package. We recognized that no one currently possessed all the commodities in its particular catalog, but we were a growing, multinational company that needed an original solution, and we believed the vendors we chose were able to think creatively.

It didn't take long for the message to sink in. A few suppliers balked and dropped by the wayside. A few others gave it a valiant effort, but couldn't quite get everything together. Finally, two viable competitors came forward with proposals. We carefully studied the resulting bid packages, asked questions of those items that appeared out of line, and, in the end, awarded an open-ended contract. In addition to a significant cost saving, the final choice reduced the five previous suppliers we were dealing with down to one.

By further discussions, we took it two steps further. First, we agreed that my company would no longer place individual purchase orders as we had in the past. Instead, we expected the supplier to keep the Kan Ban squares filled. Yet, in no case did the supplier have authorization to exceed the capacity of the product's square, not even by one box of material.

Secondly, payment would be executed upon receipt of one monthly invoice, no matter how many times product was delivered to our factory.

In this specific example, one company took over all of our packaging needs. This included everything from shipping cartons to product separators, shipping shrink wrap, all of the various shrink-sleeving our company used in its tamperproof process, the clear shrink wrap used for product grouping, and all the poly bags used to package hundreds of our products. Instead of placing hundreds of purchase orders as in the past, one person now visits the factory daily, takes inventory of the many Kan Ban squares, and schedules required product deliveries.

Today, after implementing this process with other suppliers, inventory levels are down, product shortages have been reduced, daily status meetings are history, and factory management has discovered other areas to focus on. In simple terms, it is a very successful program, and it continues to this day. The process was so successful that it continues to be expanded to other areas, with the expected benefit of reducing the total cost of acquisition while reducing the number of vendors that we do business with.

It's Not Just Big-Ticket Items

Look into other areas for vendor consolidation opportunities. Some ideas that come quickly to mind are office supplies, machine parts, hardware, formed sheet metal, and labels. Determine the total grouping of like items; find their individual annual usage, current price, and current vendor. The parameter for like items should be a loose relationship in a broad category, such as machine turning, and not specific, such as three-inch hard steel. Put a quote package together and set up an introductory meeting with your most likely suppliers to begin the process.

When the quotes are received, you need only look to the high-volume items to get a comparison to current price. This will give you a quick sanity check. Look then to the total package price. You may find a line item or two with higher costs, but if the complete package is lower than the current summation of all the various vendors in use today, then you have a strong case for consolidating vendors. In this process you will find that the total indirect costs of managing orders to a number of suppliers has been reduced. The sweetener is in achieving an overall purchase price reduction for the items.

It's Not Just Parts

Another creative approach to the vendor consolidation process concerns the delivery of materials.

If you have a chain of local suppliers, all within reasonable distance of your plant, try putting them on a regular shipping schedule. This is not as difficult as it might first appear. By having access to your detailed requirements, they can plan and build for your needs. In Chapter 13, you will read about the electronic sharing of forecasts and data in more detail.

The simplicity here is in the delivery. Make arrangements with a local trucking company to set up a regularly scheduled loop to visit each of these suppliers. The trucker will pick up whatever product is due, and by making multiple pickups, will make the transportation process more efficient. From your company's standpoint, where before there were many, now only one truck will be backing up to the receiving dock, leaving only one trailer to be unloaded.

In this variant on vendor consolidation, transportation costs are down at the same time that communications and product scheduling has improved. From your standpoint, you always know what day your vendor is scheduled to have material at your facility.

The Consolidation Process

One way of beginning vendor consolidations is to use the quoting process (discussed above).

Another process to consider, and one that is of a more strategic approach, is to stratify your suppliers according to the criteria important to your company. Some criteria might include how critical their process is to your company's success, price, and quality. In addition, you should consider their proximity, the breadth of products they offer, and their responsiveness to your needs. Determine the two or three most important components of doing business with a vendor, and then rank them in order of magnitude. Give each component a weighted average of criticality, and then assign a rank to each supplier using these criteria.

Many companies undertake this task by including other resource departments within the company, such as engineering, manufacturing, and quality personnel. The goal is to rank your suppliers, with an "A" being a top-quality, certified, and prime vendor. "B" suppliers are good performers overall, usually very reliable, and their quality performance is acceptable to excellent. "C" suppliers are not up to this level, and they are candidates to be removed from the supplier rolls over time.

If a supplier is a "C" and shows little hope of improving, then over time it needs to be culled from the list of active suppliers. Vendors such as these are costing you money, and your goal as sourcing specialist is to continuously look for the least costly, most efficient suppliers out there with whom to do business.

The "Ds" are identified as overall poor performers, and plans should be made to move them off the current vendor roll as quickly as is practical.

Look to your "B" vendors next. These are the fence sitters. The test here is to determine whether they can achieve a certified status, will remain where they are, or will drop to a "C." You are looking to decide whether they have the desire, commitment, and capability to grow to a higher performance level in your supplier chain. Do they have the potential to become a very significant partner to your company? If yes, then begin working with them, explain your goals, and encourage them to understand the means and expectations for improvement.

Keep in mind there are legitimate reasons a supplier may not get to an "A" status, and that, under certain circumstances, it would be perfectly acceptable. A supplier may not wish to invest the resources, time, and money required to achieve your goals and expectations. It may be content with its current strategy and customer base, and see no need to improve to meet your requirements. It might also be a large company, and your business is so small as to not represent a significant concern to them. Lastly, they may not understand the need for change, and may naturally be reluctant to get on board.

All of these are valid positions, made and faced up to by companies every day. The trick is for you to understand the particular circumstances involved and take the appropriate action.

Your first decision regarding the unchanging "B" supplier is whether you can continue to live with its current performance level. The criticality of the provided item, total cost, supplier location, and overall quality performance are items to be addressed and answered.

If your business relationship is such that it can continue as is for the foreseeable future, then you may be content to allow for business as usual, making sure you keep a wary eye out for performance changes. Other mitigating circumstances might play a part in your decision. There may be a limited product life, and no other future demand, making it not worth the effort to certify the supplier. A long-term relationship could be at stake, one you would want to delicately ease out of over a period of time. There could be a family business involved, with the owner reaching out to retirement in the future.

The point is that because a vendor doesn't choose to be an "A" supplier is not solid justification for it to be dropped from your vendor rolls.

Rules Governing Vendor Size

There are a few simple goals of vendor consolidation:

- ❑ Consolidate your business under one roof. This way you become more important to a supplier, and you are able to exert more influence, as needed.
- ❑ Never allow your business to exceed a given percentage of your supplier's business, usually 20 percent to 25 percent.
- ❑ Expect your supplier to grow his other business at such a rate that it maintains the relationship, noted above.

As your business grows, it is much easier to deal with a smaller population of vendors. As you develop relationships, you will experience opportunities to explore new avenues and products with your suppliers, even to the point of investing in areas not directly related to the previous core business. Vendors will be more likely to share new products and technology with you, understanding that your success is a significant part of their success. Lastly, class "A" vendors will be anxious to bring you new business opportunities they create.

Summary

Vendor consolidation does not imply that a number of your vendors are inferior, or that they supply defective product. It is only a step toward more effective sourcing for the long term.

Vendor consolidation makes good sense in the changing business climate of the twenty-first century. Not only are there the obvious cost benefits derived from larger economies of scale, but also intrinsic benefits that result from mutual support. When faced with the changes and competitive pressures of the new economy, putting all your eggs in one sourcing basket makes a lot of sense. Vendor consolidation is not a task to be lightly undertaken, and it will not be successful if it is done in a haphazard, poorly thought-out process. But when it is carefully planned for, the benefits, both quantifiable and nonquantifiable, are significant.

CHAPTER 6

Vendor Performance

YOU CAN FINALLY KICK BACK and relax a bit. The vendor of choice has been determined, the site visits are completed, the product is qualified, the cost reductions are in and very attractive, the long-term understanding is in place, and the vendor-managed inventory process is up and running. Everything looks good, and your work is done.

I hope you don't really believe this.

The best price possible, with less than optimal quality or delivery performance, is not the basis of an acceptable agreement. Unless all three legs on the milking stool are solid—price, performance, and quality, the stool is broken and you will eventually be unceremoniously dumped where you'd rather not be.

The lesson is that the deal is never done.

A Measure of Success

In an effective partnership, both parties take the pulse of the business on a regular basis. Performance must be measured, and the results must be evaluated. Proper facilitation begins with clear and accurate information.

Regular communication and feedback from both parties are vital requirements. The seller will want to know whether the original fore-cast numbers are being met or exceeded. Is the market changing in any appreciable manner, especially in a way that might create a de-mand for a new product or process? Are there increasing opportuni-ties over the horizon, or is a product in decline, necessitating a future reduction in demand? Straight answers to these critical questions en-sure that your supplier is privy to what it needs to know to be your confident, successful partner.

At the same time, there are very specific measurements you as the buyer need to create and monitor to ensure that the basics of the agreement are in place and continue to make business sense. Your agreement should clearly spell out some common definitions by which both companies can communicate and operate.

On-Time Delivery

What is considered on time when it comes to product delivery at your site? Consider this carefully, particularly if you are dealing with global sources.

For example, it is not uncommon for a remote supplier, such as a manufacturing company located in China, in all good faith, to believe that the date on your order is its date to deliver product to the freight forwarder or shipper, not the date you are expecting it to arrive on your dock. This one-line misunderstanding will adversely impact your product availability schedules.

In Japan in the 1970s, JIT and Kan Ban manufacturing were rap-idly coming on stream and beginning to prove their operational bene-fits. It was common for large automobile manufacturers to schedule vendor deliveries, directly to the consuming floor location, with a plus or minus delivery window of fifteen minutes. Material delivered too early was considered a performance failure, and just as serious as being too late.

This may be a bit stringent by U.S. manufacturing standards, but an expected delivery window should be created and performance against that window should be measured. Material delivered too early increases the risk of quality and obsolescence issues, and just as im-portant, impacts cash flow by creating a financial liability sooner than necessary.

Material delivered late runs the risk of creating shortages on the factory floor, slowing or stopping the manufacturing process. The impact of a line being stopped includes the cost of the idled labor, unabsorbed fixed overhead cost, inventory investment, and delay to your customers. These are nonrecoverable, sunk costs.

Sourcing personnel are key players in the team effort to balance costs of early inventory investment against the costs associated with a stopped manufacturing line.

The delivery situation is different in the United States, where suppliers are spread across the continent but the communications and support infrastructure is more reliable. A factor to be considered in the vendor evaluation and qualification process is location and proximity to your plant. The closer the vendor is to your plant, the easier it is to maintain reduced inventory levels, more frequent deliveries, improved quality, and effective communication.

It might be reasonable to schedule inventory arrivals to something like a one- or two-day early, zero-days late criteria, at least for domestic suppliers. This is a starting point. Anything delivered in this window can be considered to have been on time. Anything outside this window has not been delivered on time, and will be measured and reported accordingly.

When a critical supplier is half a world away, scheduling becomes dicier. Significant cost reductions available in the Far East must be weighed carefully with the realities of a more complex, yet weaker, support structure. It is impossible to adhere to strict delivery schedules. In addition, there is a required cost and inventory investment when planning for the variances associated with loading containers at the factory, delivering them to a transport ship, a three-week passage on the ocean, unloading and handling, potential labor issues, increasingly stringent customs and security requirements, and, finally, inbound freight.

For these reasons, most companies open a somewhat wider window on delivery acceptability when dealing with a distant supplier, and use different criteria to measure offshore versus domestic production.

Partnership in Reducing Inventory

Increasingly, sophisticated planning and process controls will reduce on-hand inventory levels and improve customer response times, while significantly reducing stock-out, quality, and obsolescence risks. Inventory investment is affected by delivery frequency and lot sizes. Creative ways to reduce inventories should be actively pursued. If zero-inventory levels with minute-by-minute deliveries are at one end of the spectrum, then anything beyond that increases the risks. Although daily deliveries, for example, might be impractical at first, increasing the frequency of deliveries always reduces inventory investment and risk.

Data Accuracy

Constantly improving accuracy and performance must be uppermost in the minds of today's sourcing specialist. Data measurements must be in place. The type of data measured ranges from packing slip and invoice accuracy to actual counts of material delivered, number of packages, correct part numbers, descriptions, and order numbers.

The Next Wave

When it comes to measuring vendor performance, there is a new wave building. The momentum is turning toward measuring on-time performance, not to its commitment or to our requirements, but to the customer need date. This is a radical concept and the next significant step toward performance improvement. Few companies are in a position to measure it correctly today, fewer still are geared to use the information garnered, but it is where industry is headed. Start thinking about it.

This is not an easy project, and it will require a significant investment in electronic data interface capabilities far beyond the capabilities of most suppliers and customers today. In the end, the vendor will see the customer's point-of-sale data and be in a position to quickly react to it. This is twenty-first century sourcing at it finest.

Correct Documentation

Correct documentation is imperative, regardless of the media. In this section, documentation refers to actual paperwork, such as purchase orders, receiving documents, invoices, and packing slips, along with data transferred by an electronic medium. The means of transmission is of much less importance than the accuracy of the data involved.

One of the operating criteria within your company should be that all invoices that are not completely correct must be reviewed. Subsequently, corrective action must be taken by the sourcing specialist, who will also be charged with reporting this against vendor performance.

Pay particular attention to pricing. Innocent and some not-so-innocent changes can occur, resulting in an erroneous price being charged your company. If the price is too high, you are overpaying, and if it is too low, your supplier is faced with not making the margin it expects. In both cases, a good sourcing specialist will address the question and get it corrected immediately.

A three-pronged check and security process is the most common practice these days, and one highly recommended. A purchase document is matched with a receiving transaction and a separate invoice. This dictates that each and every receipt is accompanied by a packing slip, which creates the inventory transactions, which creates an invoice, and so on. Any disparity is reason to stop all transactions, investigate the error, determine the corrective action, and not continue until it is resolved.

The same criteria hold for the involved documentation. Constantly having to correct recurring errors on vendor paperwork (such as wrong prices, incorrect delivered or ordered quantities, wrong orders, or incorrect shipping addresses) is a valid reason to reject the process, and count against vendor performance, as already noted. Problems such as these are an added cost of doing business with a particular vendor. They create non-value-added activities, and must be considered in the total cost equation. A vendor's performance regarding correct documentation is just as important as its on-time and quality measurement results. You should expect documentation to be complete, correct, and on time. Anything less is measured and reported.

Quality

The 1980s brought about a concerted push in the quality arena, driven by the perception that the Japanese were far and away the leaders in manufacturing due to their edge in product quality. W.

Edwards Deming and Joseph Juran were viewed as the leaders in the quality movement, each sending a message more respected in Japan than in their own country.

For a while, the marching order was for Zero Defects, followed closely by the more popular Quality Circles. Individual departments within thousands of companies started these Quality Circle teams. Each group of employees was empowered to look at product or process issues, and make recommendations to management with the goal of improving quality and reducing costs. Philip Crosby was a leader in this movement. His book *Quality Is Free* became a manufacturing bible, making obligatory appearances on most business leaders' bookshelves.[1]

Like other mantras that originally boiled over under the heat of management focus and then simmered down with time, quality has been receiving a reduced level of attention of late. This is due to significant improvements in the manufacturing arena, as companies have continually enhanced their perceived quality to meet rising customer expectations.

What you are striving for is a quality level in your product that meets customer needs and expectations, but is not overkill. Correct quality performance is what is required, not what is technically possible. As a sourcing specialist, you face a delicate balance between overpaying for quality you don't need, and underpaying for quality that you do.

It is important that your supplier clearly understands your company's expectations, process requirements, and specifications, and is able to meet them in a timely and reasonable manner. If it plans to supply you with something of a significantly better quality level than your specifications might require, you probably will pay too much. You are also overpaying, regardless of a lower purchase price, if there are regular lot rejections due to quality levels from your supplier not meeting your needs. In both cases, product is costing you more than it should.

Measure quality. Measure incoming performance. Expecting 98.5 percent or 99.5 percent as an incoming minimum threshold is not out of the question these days, and, in fact, might be considered as the lower limit of acceptability.

Both parties should understand that a single reject could reject the whole lot. "One bad, all bad" is reasonable in today's world of sourcing. You are paying for the right product at the right price. A vendor should be expected to check and certify its work. If the vendor is doing the job it should, there is no reason you should double-check it or sort the results.

Packaging

A global sourcing specialist must also become something of an expert in correct packaging. Products shipped long distances are susceptible to an additional risk of damage that locally supplied materials may not be. However, the contents of a well-packed container, loaded at the vendor site, and never opened until being unloaded at your dock, should have no damage. In shipping, packaging material is dead weight; something paid for, taking up space, but not actually consumed as direct material. Therefore, you must demand the correct level of packaging to provide adequate protection to your goods to ensure they arrive in an undamaged condition. At the same time, you must balance the cost and performance with the price of paying for dead weight and occupying rented space, which brings no added value to your product and process.

Vendor Certification

If your company does not have a vendor certification process in place, it should consider starting one, and sourcing is the department to lead the effort. (See Chapter 7.) As a customer and potential partner, you should visit your vendor at its factory site and look at all aspects of its operation to ensure it can do what it claims and has the equipment, processes, tools, and personnel required to support your needs. Vendor sourcing and factory visits are discussed in more detail in Chapter 9.

I recommend that you consider as certified any company that has gone through the effort and expense to receive a recognized quality certification, such as the Baldrige National Quality Award, ISO 9001, or the automotive QS 9000 quality certification.[2] You are taking minimal risks by assuming they can meet your needs and do the job correctly. You should still do the initial site visit and survey, but in less detail. Don't waste a significant amount of time and effort doing the work that others, who are much more qualified, have already completed for you.

Summary

Finalizing and implementing the vendor agreement is only one step on the road to successful sourcing in the twenty-first century. It is neither a destination nor a final accomplishment. Successful relationships are built on continued and open communication, mutual trust, and quantitative data. Performance measurements must be in place and understood and reviewed. Action must be taken on the results. The total cost of acquisition must be known and understood, as it is more important than purchase price alone.

There are many performance criteria that should be measured and reported on, some of which are discussed in this chapter. The potential list is significantly longer, but those identified are a good set to begin with. It is also important to know that consistency of measurement is more important than sophistication. Measuring an unmanageable number of variables becomes nonproductive, especially when it is more important to simply know one particular item is rejected more frequently than another.

Unless the movement is toward constant improvement, status quo means falling behind. Like any successful system implementation, striving for constant improvement can only be made when you understand where you are and where you need to be.

Notes

1. Philip Crosby, *Quality Is Free: The Art of Making Quality Certain* (New York: McGraw-Hill, 1979).
2. For information on the Baldrige National Quality Award, visit the Web site of the National Institute of Standards and Technology at www.quality.nist.gov. For information on the ISOO 9001, visit the Web site of the International Organization for Standardization at www.iso.ch. For information on QS9000, visit the Web site of the American Society for Quality at www.asq.org or qs9000.asq.org.

CHAPTER 7

Vendor Certification

THE FACT THAT PRICE ALONE is a poor indicator of vendor performance should be clear by now. It is only one leg of the three-legged stool consisting of price, performance, and quality, and only one part of the sourcing specialist's criteria for doing business with a particular vendor.

Any critical, long-term business relationship should include vendor certification, which will yield a clearer understanding of the strengths and weaknesses of your supplier. With this information at hand, you are able to build on the strong points of your supplier's skills while avoiding the traps and pitfalls of potentially weak areas.

The Scope of Vendor Certification

The first steps in the certification process are to be sure you understand what the term means, the criteria for measurement, how the process is implemented, and what the expected outcomes are. It would be wise to have a mission statement to share with your potential partners to ensure they understand your needs and why you are asking them to open their doors to the process.

Certification is a process of quantifying the significant processes within a vendor's organization. By tallying the results and comparing them to a perfect score, your company should be able to determine the probability of how well a supplier will be able to meet your requirements.

An effective certification process should cover all aspects of doing business with that supplier, including manufacturing process controls, quality control, sales order processing, traffic, inventory control, and customer service, among others. It is a sliding scale, with a means of assigning a numeric value to key functions within a company. It weighs their impact upon your operation and comes up with a final score. Many of the judgments that go into achieving the score are subjective, but the number becomes a way to quantitatively measure a variety of functions at your supplier and to set up your supplier on a tiered program for comparative purposes.

When conducting the vendor survey, you should look at as many aspects of the company processes as possible. Generally, a team should visit the site, with the expectation of spending a few hours in each of the identified areas. The team should have detailed questions about how each process works. It should ask to see representative samples of paperwork and procedures, and try to identify potentially weak areas that might adversely affect business with your company. The team should also know the experiences to date with the supplier in terms of delivery performance and ongoing quality.

When beginning a vendor certification process, there are other notes to keep in mind. Do not expect to certify every supplier on your vendor list, and do not expect every surveyed company to attain an acceptable score. As a smaller company, you cannot afford the undertaking in the first case, and it is naive to expect universal passing results in the second. Finally, the benefits of certification are on a sliding scale. The return on the investment in time and money in certifying smaller vendors could be far outweighed by the costs involved in conducting the survey.

Who Should Be Certified?

A standard process should be established for determining under what conditions a vendor would or even must be considered for certification. It goes without saying that a documented process must exist in your company for vendor evaluation and certification. Create the process and obtain buy-in from the significant functions within your company before attempting to begin the certification process with your partners.

A vendor should not be considered for the evaluation and certification process if it supplies only commodity, off-the-shelf-type items, easily available in a standardized form from a number of suppliers. A quick example might be hardware.

Vendors already certified by an acceptable outside review process or industry standard can be exempted from the evaluation and certification process. Some examples of industry standards include companies certified under the ISO 9000 series of standards. National Baldrige Quality Award winners should also be exempted from your process. Your company must make a decision as to the level of assumed quality to be expected by suppliers certified under an outside agency or recognized quality standard, but in the beginning of the vendor certification process, assume these vendors will meet your needs, and move on to other companies that will yield you a better return for the time and effort you invest with them.

A more realistic candidate for evaluation and certification would be a supplier who manufacturers a very critical, one-of-a-kind product, or a vendor who requires a significant, up-front investment in tooling, for example.

In determining candidates for certification, you might also consider the following:

❑ **The Impact Upon Your Company's Success.** If a candidate is a sole source for a very critical component of your product, then it is a prime candidate for certification.

❑ **The Level of Purchase Dollars Spent with a Vendor.** This one is a little tricky. If you are spending a large amount of sourcing dollars with a supplier, but are buying an off-the-shelf commodity, there probably is little reason to certify that supplier. If the dollars spent are significant, and the component unique or to your specifications, then a certification visit is in order.

❑ **Unique Technology.** If the vendor you have or one being courted offers a unique technology or process that your company is considering for current or future products, it should be a serious survey candidate. This is especially true if your company is going to invest significant design efforts into utilizing this product.

❑ **The Long-Term Impact of the Product Offered.** If the item offered is critical to your product and will be used for an appreciable amount of time into the future, then the vendor should be certified.

❑ **The Significant Potential Cost Savings with a New Product or Vendor.** We are all on the lookout for potential purchase cost or labor savings. If a supplier becomes known who offers a significant cost savings with a new process or product, and your company feels confident about it, then the vendor should be certified.

The Certification Team

Once a process is in place to determine certification candidates, and the certification process identified, the next step is to determine the makeup of the certification team.

Sourcing personnel must be team leaders. They are responsible for all aspects of vendor relations, and they need to be viewed as the point organization in all vendor activities. The next most important team members must support the requirements of quality and engineering. Additional requirements from marketing and finance should also be considered.

Recommendations and reasons for certifying vendors can originate in any department within the organization, but the final plan, schedule, arrangements, and team members should be strongly influenced by sourcing.

A standard certification procedure and separate rating sheet and summary document are required. The procedure deals with how the process is done. The rating document ideally will be a multipage checklist to use in evaluating all relevant functions within a potential supplier's operation. It lists the functions to be addressed, the questions to be asked, the processes to be investigated, and the suggested performance numbers, based upon the outcome.

What the Survey Should Look For

As part of the certification process, you need to have a clear understanding of the traits you should be looking for.

The first step with a potential supplier is to gain an understanding of its process in making the widgets your company is interested in. Mentally and verbally identify several questions to ensure your needs to understand the company are addressed, and make note of your personal observations and hunches. A few questions to include are:

- ❑ **Is the plant efficient?** Modern equipment and efficiency often go hand-in-hand, but realize there are very efficient, cost-effective plants around the world with very little in the way of modern equipment. A skilled workman can do amazing things with a leather-driven lathe.
- ❑ **What kind of quality system is in place?** ISO 9001, for example, is wonderful exercise, and the training is excellent. Certified plants from one of several organizations are also exceptional indicators, but a plant without these certifications is not necessarily inferior. The important point is that the potential supplier understands its process and knows how to measure and control it.
- ❑ **What are employee relations like?** Are people encouraged to partake in plant decisions, make customer quality recommendations, and attend regular plant meetings that address performance improvements, cost savings, and efficiencies?
- ❑ **Does the supplier make arrangements to have key factory direct labor personnel visit customer facilities to learn how the parts they make are used?** After such a visit, it is not unusual to experience an increase in quality, based on people who finally learn and understand how the part they make is used in your operation, and why the specifications are what they are.
- ❑ **Does the supplier make the effort to thoroughly understand its customer's needs and expectations?**
- ❑ **Does the supplier know who the end users are and what forces are being exerted upon them?**
- ❑ **Does it make the effort to understand its supplier's needs?**
- ❑ **What is upstream and how can it help make its suppliers successful?**
- ❑ **What is the supplier's vendor quality improvement program like?**

Other members of the survey team will address similar questions in other departments. For example, the sales order process used by a vendor needs to be reviewed and understood. Team members need to question:

- ❏ How are back orders treated?
- ❏ What is the invoicing process?
- ❏ What checks exist in the system to verify that customer service criteria are met?
- ❏ How is the customer notified of late/partial shipments?
- ❏ How are routings verified?
- ❏ Is there an internal audit process?
- ❏ Is there a customer follow-up process?
- ❏ How is customer performance measured?
- ❏ How is customer quality measured?
- ❏ How is customer quality reported?

Again, these are just a few areas that can and should be looked at. Team brainstorming will determine the questions most appropriate for your company to ask.

Engineering and quality will get into their respective areas and ask similar questions. Topics should include technical design competence, repeatability in manufacturing processes, state of the design and quality tools, performance measurements, product specifications, ongoing quality checks, and customer satisfaction.

Measuring and Scoring Results

You can take many approaches to the scoring process, all of which, if carefully thought out, will be measurements of activities required to meet your company's needs. The absolute, final numeric score is less important as a measurement or report card than as a comparative tool used to rank a vendor in relation to other vendors. Seriously consider limiting the range of numbers used for measurement. Having a scoring range of one through ten might be excessive, as it is difficult to differentiate between a rating of six or seven, for example. A one to five range will be more than adequate for your needs, and successful programs have run on a zero, one, three, and five scale.

Each functional area should have its own weighting in the overall scheme. For example, in a very technical process, such as critical machining of a part, or a process that has a high-yield fluctuation, the weighting of quality might be higher than order processing. If your process requires a lot of deliveries, then correct order processing and the traffic functions might be more important. The goal is to identify the functions that most affect your company, and weigh them in accordingly.

Each operation looked at within a function should be scored. Of the eight items I identified regarding a factory visit at the beginning of this piece, each should be individually rated, and a sum should be determined for the function.

Each function identified should be scored separately, and a sum determined. This is then divided by the total possible score, to yield a performance percentage for that department. The result is multiplied by its weighting factor. The results for all departments are added to get a total score, which cannot exceed one hundred.

For example, the eight modules in manufacturing are each scored from one to five, and their sum might add up to twenty-six. Twenty-six divided by the total possible score of forty equals 65 percent. Below is how this might look on the questionnaire tabulation:

Item	Score	Ideal Score
1) Plant efficiency	3	5
2) Quality system	4	5
3) Employee relations	4	5
4) Customer visits	1	5
5) Customer needs	3	5
6) Secondary customer needs	3	5
7) Supplier needs	4	5
8) Vendor quality improvement	4	5
Total manufacturing score	26	40
Manufacturing percentage	26/40 = 65%	

Coincidentally, sales order processing also had eight questions, so its best possible score would be forty in this example. If accounts receivable only had six measurements, its possible score would be thirty, and so on through each process. In the end, all functions are then added together and divided by the total possible score to yield an overall result.

Putting the Results to Use

Each company will have to decide how it wishes to rate suppliers, but consider the following suggestions. Until you get several of these rating experiences under your belt, treat your efforts as research only, and decide on the ranges of acceptable certification only at some future date. Initially, it might feel necessary to create an artificial cutoff of acceptability, say 60 percent. It will only be after you have completed a few certification surveys that you will get a sense of how realistic your rating system is.

Certification of your vendors covers a lot of territory, and what is suggested here is more an outline upon which to build than an absolute, definitive plan. However, if your current company does not have such a plan in place, the performance return dictates that it is more important that the process begin quickly than that every last detail is worked out.

On a longer-term basis, you might wish to share comparative data with your suppliers. It might prove very helpful at negotiation time to provide a vendor with its survey results comparing it to other surveyed suppliers, comparing its score to your larger vendor population. In cases where it might be necessary to convince your suppliers to support the certification process, and to work toward constantly improving their performance, you might offer that vendors who achieve a certain level score may be considered certified. Thus, they can expect less stringent incoming inspection or more favorable payment terms.

Summary

Certification is a means to identify and understand your critical vendors, know their processes and functions, and help ensure that they can meet your current and future needs without undue risk to your business. It is also a tool to quantitatively compare one vendor to another. It can be used in the total cost of acquisition analysis, discussed later in this book, as a factor of purchase price. The point is that vendor certification is a process gaining in importance in this century, and a tool the modern sourcing specialist will want to be well acquainted with.

This is by no means a comprehensive list of components a good sourcing person should be checking for, nor necessarily the best way to construct the survey process, but it is a good beginning to the thought process and the considerations of a vendor certification program.

Kill Paper, Not Trees

CLEARLY, SOURCING SPECIALISTS TODAY have moved well beyond being mere order placers. Forward-thinking organizations have relegated the weekly drudgery of placing hundreds of purchase orders with countless suppliers to a distant memory. It has become a process as outdated as Kardex files. Handling all this paper is wasted, non-value-added effort, yielding no return on the human capital invested by the twenty-first century company.

Redirecting time spent placing orders toward efforts at finding the absolute best supplier for your commodity, the one willing to provide the right product, at the right quality, on time, and at the best total cost, is a much more effective utilization of you as a resource. By applying the knowledge you are gaining with this book, you will have the opportunity to save your company thousands of dollars in wasteful processes and time-consuming, inefficient practices. Every dollar saved in this manner drops directly to the bottom line, a measurement that anyone can understand.

Paperless Inventory Management

In Chapter 5, I talked about one manufacturing company that annually consumed tens of thousands of cartons, in hundreds of sizes, for products it supplied to the consumer market. As good manufacturing processes require, each had a part number, and each was forecasted and run through the MRP system. Annual usage quantities varied from the hundreds to the tens of thousands.

In meeting the goals that sourcing should be striving for today, only one purchase order was placed with the packaging partner. The order had one line that read something like "packaging," and a figure for a dollar amount probably made up based upon the phase of the moon. It was there just to be entered into the master computer system.

Vendor-managed inventory was a new function implemented in this factory at the same time the packaging agreement was finalized. In lieu of detailed requirements, whether via forecast or actual lines on a purchase order, the supplier was charged with managing its customer's inventory.

By instituting this process in one factory, we reduced the amount of packing slips, invoices, and computer transactions from literally hundreds per month, in some cases, to two. It doesn't get any easier, cheaper, and certainly not more efficient than this.

Researching Opportunities

The institution of this process is not as easy as I may have suggested, nor as difficult as it might seem. It takes dedicated effort and planning by all departments involved, including production, planning, sourcing, and accounting. Agreement needs to be reached on the details and the transactions required, the minimum and maximum lot sizes to be in the Kan Ban squares, and the responsibility for managing the steps in the process.

The savings in labor, handling, and storage makes it well worth the effort. Vendor-managed inventory is also a natural for other high-labor, low-return functions for which sourcing is typically responsible.

For example, ordering office supplies is an area ripe for this level of management. The process here is simple. Gather up all the data you can on annual consumption of the largest-value products, such as copy paper, writing instruments, and toner cartridges. These high-volume, high-value items will be indicative of the total dollars involved in the quote.

Put the list out for quote to a few of the major industry suppliers, and don't be too concerned if most of the numbers come back pretty close to each other. Typically, this business is very competitive, and the margins at the supplier level are razor thin. What you are really looking to procure here is service.

Will the companies deliver to your central storeroom? Will they deliver the heavy boxes of copy paper directly to the consuming areas? How frequently will they deliver? Will they determine the replacement orders, and keep your shelves properly stocked?

These functions are labor-intensive for your company personnel, and if a vendor is willing to take them on as part of the deal, then sign on.

Don't stop at office supplies. Look to your MRO (Maintenance, Repair, and Operations) buys and maintenance support for additional opportunities.

In the case of maintenance and MRO purchases, it likely is more difficult to arrange for vendors to manage all of the products required, usually because of the diversity of the needs and the infrequency of ordering. In these cases, it might be best to provide individual purchase orders.

But opportunities to save exist even under these circumstances. The first step is to consolidate the number of possible vendors, as we have already discussed. The second step is to utilize those suppliers who have electronic order entry capabilities. In these cases, you will obtain cost reductions for your company by exercising the ability to enter your order through a Web site, obtaining the price and delivery date, verifying availability, and obtaining shipping information in one set of keystrokes.

Don't leave any stone unturned in your search for improved processes. The numbers supporting the total cost savings and improved efficiency will substantiate the effort in electronic order placement or setting up vendor-managed inventory whenever possible, regardless of the product.

Chasing the Butterflies While the Elephants Escape

While we're studying old processes and assumptions, let's address another hard-to-kill sacred cow.

Chasing elephants and butterflies is a contraction of Pareto's law: A minority of input produces the majority of results.[1] Vilfredo Pareto

(1848-1923) was an Italian engineer and economist who came up with this theory in relation to the distribution of wealth.

Often referred to as the 80:20 rule, or at times, elephants and butterflies, it says that 20 percent of your effort yields 80 percent of the results, and 80 percent of your effort yields a 20 percent return. This stratification works toward customers, inventory levels, purchase orders, and most anything else you can compare.

In other words, while you are spending time chasing the butterflies through the skies, the elephants are escaping. Focus on the big things, and the little ones will take care of themselves.

All orders placed for direct materials are the result of a factory plan. The sophisticated companies may use a precise, industry-accepted process called Sales and Operations Planning (S. & O.P.), or a similar derivative. Whatever the process used, the purpose is to get the key departments including marketing, sales, finance, manufacturing, and the executive staff together to agree on the company's future production, sales, and financial plans. This is not a detailed document covering the next thirty days, but a long-range definition of broader goals and the production and sales numbers that support them.

At these review meetings, marketing will discuss future opportunities, sales current orders, and new possibilities. Manufacturing might address capacity issues, and finance might provide the numbers documenting how all of the above will be paid for and the expectations for what will fall to the bottom line. The last step is for executive staff to sign off on the final document.

From the sourcing perspective, all direct material purchases are driven from this high-level plan, which all key departments and functions have created and accepted. Since the executive staff has given the plan its stamp of approval, I question the value of requiring inventory purchase orders to be approved and signed off by ever-increasing levels of authority, depending upon their total dollar value. The top managers have already signed for the plan; why do they need to sign for the details?

As a member of today's cadre of sourcing specialists, you are a professional, constantly striving to improve. You are well trained, and driven to succeed. Your personal and professional goals and objectives are clear. The measurements of performance are concise, quantifiable, and understood. What you don't need is another nonvalue-added obstacle, like someone looking over your shoulder, second-guessing your work. In this instance, I feel better about my company when the executives are managing the elephants, while I take care of the butterflies.

Electronic Business

Much of supply chain management, which is the current term in vogue for aligning supply with requirements, lends itself to hands-off, automatic processing. Machines talking to machines, handling the monotonous transactions that make up the majority of supplier-to-customer business activities, makes perfect sense. Routine and repetitive ordering and selling, encompassing standard terms and conditions, is something machines can do quite well, usually with less opportunity for error than human interfaces.

Electronic purchase orders are a natural for MRO and maintenance orders. Automatic invoicing, keystroke money transfers, and online query capabilities are all techniques and processes that improve efficiency and reduce direct labor in the repetitive tasks of daily business. The modern company needs to invest financial and human capital in a wise and efficient manner, a manner leading to the opportunity for the greatest return.

There is zero return to be had from repetitive, nonvalue-added paperwork. Putting systems in place to handle the routine goes a long way toward freeing a buyer's time to work on the important issues that cross her desk daily. Replacing these time-consuming transactions with those requiring the special attention that a human can apply will yield measurably improved results to the total organizational efficiency.

Another function where the lives of thousands of trees will be spared is invoicing. Most companies create a packing slip for every shipment they make to a customer. Many of their internal systems, whether electronic or manual, will at the same time create an invoice, which is then sent to the customer, reflecting the contents of that packing slip. A company that supplies a number of shipments to a customer can end up generating a handful of invoices each week.

A growing number of companies accumulate information and send only one monthly invoice, contributing to their efficiency while attaining indirect cost reductions. Just as it costs extra to handle the excess invoices at the receiving end, so is it an expense to generate the documents at the supplier side.

Forward-thinking companies are taking the next step by allowing for electronic invoicing and funds transfers. As in other areas, the preparatory work required is not to be overlooked, but the end results in indirect cost savings can be substantial.

The process accumulates all of the invoicing information for an agreed-upon time, such as a month. At an agreed date, the invoice is released electronically into the customer's account. Through an internal matching software transaction, the customer's system agrees with the invoice and releases funds for payment. Additional paper trail and cost reductions occur when, instead of a check being written, mailed, and then handled at the vendor's site, funds are transferred electronically. Once again, the routine of matching packing slip, receipt transaction, and invoice is removed from the desk of the accounts payable clerk and put into capable electronic hands.

It should be clear that, whether you are planning materials, placing orders, or paying the monthly organizational bills, the goal is to allow the electronic system to process the routine majority of transactions in any organization. The advantages of a simple-minded computer are that it never gets bored, doesn't require breaks or days off, is very good at the basics of repetitive processing, and can't be beat on a cost-per-transaction basis.

While we are on the topic of electronic communications, there are a number of other opportunities for machines to talk to each other, sparing the lives of a few more trees.

For many routine communications, e-mail is a wonderful mode of asking and answering questions, documenting plans and actions, and creating a nonpaper trail. It does not replace the benefits of face-to-face meetings, where body language is an integral part of effective communication. Nor does it replace a telephone call, where tone and inflection are keys to effective communication. But properly used as a medium for less stringent messages, it is ideal.

Another cost saver is using e-mail to transmit documents. Why type, print, and mail a memo, when e-mail will do? When a separate document is required, it is more cost-effective to send it as an attachment, allowing the receiver to decide the need of printing it versus reading and storing it online. The benefits of electronically sending detailed engineering drawings and specifications, flow charts, photographs, and artwork are obvious, not only in the paper and labor savings associated with printing, handling, mailing, or priority shipments, but also in the instant feedback on questions and clarifications. Decisions that might have previously required days or weeks can be made in hours.

Summary

As you read through this book, you will find many references to killing paperwork. Sometimes this is a difficult task, as much of it was previously believed a required part of the job. Just as I have tried to demonstrate the waste of time and dollars in processing hundreds of purchase order documents, packing slips, invoices, and receipts, look for other areas where reports and flows might easily be replaced by more efficient means. New opportunities for efficiency are not always obvious, but they are worth digging out.

Note

1. www.paretolaw.co.uk/principle.html.

CHAPTER 9

Knowledge Is Power

THIS OLD CHESTNUT is a cornerstone in the world of professional sourcing. There is a strong correlation between product knowledge, training, and your value as a sourcing specialist. As you become more knowledgeable, you will become more effective, and the faster you will progress along your desired career path.

The purchasing job track usually begins on a lower rung of the department, with promotions linked to a growing level of knowledge and experience.[1] Internal training covers the intricacies of the company, the functional departments and their responsibilities, the products sold, and the company history, including its strengths and weaknesses. You learn how to deal with customers and suppliers. With time and study, you become a more valuable contributor to the team.

Product Knowledge

In order to be a successful sourcing specialist, an important part of your knowledge base must include an understanding of your company's products and the components that go into their makeup.

You should have ready answers to these questions:

❑ How are the products purchased/made?
❑ Who are the critical suppliers?
❑ What are the significant components?
❑ Who are the major competitors?
❑ What edge does this product have over the competitor's product?

Controlling the Dissemination of Company Information

When you begin dealing directly with vendors, you might initially be surprised to discover how much they know about your business and your customers. An astonishing amount of proprietary information is out there, more than a good sourcing specialist should be comfortable with. As a successful buyer, you must be concerned with how such data gets out there, and by training and caution, make sure that you are not contributing to the problem.

One step is to always be sensitive to the ongoing questions that visitors and vendors ask regarding aspects of your company, its processes, the customer base, technology, or other areas. Never write this off as idle chatter, but instead realize that these people are likely following the professional approach of attempting to learn as much as possible about customers and competitors. How you respond is a matter between you, company policy, management, and good business sense, but always think ahead, and know where the questioner is attempting to lead you. Err on the side of caution.

Anything involving patented processes, company secrets, emerging technologies, and new markets should remain under wraps and off the general questions table. If discussed at all, these subjects can only be talked about under the protection and with the signatories of a nondisclosure agreement. Key account information should be classified the same way, especially regarding suppliers, customers, and competitors. Be sure you understand the risks in sharing information.

I once ran an interesting role-playing exercise with my staff at a medium-size manufacturing company. My role was as a possible supplier that had just entered a quote for certain products. The exercise was for the staff to conduct a follow-up meeting with the supplier, and do a mock, first-pass, negotiation session. My goal in the exercise was to determine the target price and where my proposal fit within the quoted range. Without going into all the details, by a series of innocent questions about my quote, supplier locations, and level of interest, I was easily able to ascertain the target price and who my competitors were.

The point is that my team knew my goal from the beginning and was tasked to make sure they did not give out the information, yet I was successful in obtaining it. If they were prepared for the test and still inadvertently shared the information, what can happen to a single buyer not specifically briefed ahead of time?

Think carefully and exercise good business sense. There are a few simple rules that, if followed, will help ensure data integrity.

❏ **Never share a competitor's price, price quote, technical details, or even its name with another competitor.** When asked, you should inform the questioner that you consider this information proprietary in nature. You may be told that the information can be easily obtained. That may be so, but you should feel confident in knowing that it will never come from you. You are also demonstrating your level of integrity by assuring the requester that you will also not be sharing its data.

❏ **Always honor information of a competitive nature.** As in pricing, this is never to be shared, under any circumstances.

❏ **Data and information created by a supplier is never to be sent directly to a competitor, under any guise.**

The goal is to remain the silent participant, and make your bidders and partners feel good in knowing that information shared with you will be kept confidential and secure.

Another consideration is to be careful when touring suppliers and others through your facility. Be especially cautious with those with whom you are not currently doing business. A vigilant, sharp-eyed vendor will learn a great deal about your business and who its competition might be just by observing product cartons and material stored on your factory floor.

A vendor can also gauge your business levels by noting activity, learn your process, and estimate your desired and actual inventory levels, all by paying close attention during an innocent factory tour.

In general, it is not a good idea to host such a tour with a supplier until you have been doing business together for a while.

When to Open Your Information Kimono

On the other hand, you should have no serious reservations about factory tours with those suppliers with whom you have had a long-term business relationship, those who have just committed to a partnership plan, and those who have agreed to run vendor-managed inventory for you.

Withholding information regarding how a chosen supplier's product is to be used will usually be counterproductive toward meeting long-range strategic and partnership goals. If your supplier is kept in the dark and not allowed to understand your needs and process, there is little it can do to help in new technology, cost reductions, or process efficiencies. If the sourcing qualification process has worked correctly, it is counterproductive to not trust your vendor with the information required to do the job correctly.

There are benefits to the sharing of information that might not be readily apparent. For example, a supplier may note an opportunity to improve a process that he observes, even in an area not directly related to his product. He might be aware of other, more efficient technologies related more to his industry than yours, but, nonetheless, having applications to your process. Just in touring other facilities, he may have ideas about how similar industries are addressing problems or coming up with innovative solutions.

In the end, it is imperative to understand that, just as you are fanatical about managing cash for your company, data and information are no less important, nor less valuable. Treat your factory floor as your company's storehouse of knowledge, and limit access to those who need to know about it, and to those who can be trusted.

Know Your Suppliers

As you know your own products and company, so should you know your suppliers. You need to understand their financial and competitive position, whether they are market leaders or followers, who their largest customers and suppliers are, and what your impact is upon their business.

The financial health of your supplier is a key indicator that you will want to learn about early on. Numerous sources of information on this subject are readily available, including Dun and Bradstreet, annual reports and stock market analyst reports from brokerage houses, along with customer and supplier references. Depending upon the magnitude of your proposed business relationship and the criticality of the supplied component to the success of your company's product, you may choose to use only one, several, or all of these investigative tools. Don't be afraid to call and talk to references, and then ask for other possible contacts. In this manner, you can create your own sources outside of the ones provided. You should know all you can about your supplier's fiscal health before entering into an exclusive partnership program.

But money is not everything. What is the supplier's competitive position? Is it the leading supplier, in the middle of the pack, or a distant follower? Being the technological leader is often an effective indicator for an extended and successful partnership arrangement. The company that invests in research and development and is seen as a market innovator by its customers, and grudgingly acknowledged as a leader by its competitors, is usually a good company to align with.

Another key area to investigate is determining who the supplier's major accounts are, and what percentage of the business it has. Generally speaking, you should be uncomfortable being more than 20 percent to 30 percent of a supplier's business. A supplier that is too dependent upon your future is exhibiting poor management technique by exposing itself to a more concentrated risk than it should. When your business experiences a significant slowdown, which can happen to any company at any time, the vendor risks laying off its workforce, or closing facilities.

In the first case, it may lose the skilled labor required to continue producing your product. In the latter, you will have lost the key supplier for a component. As a professional sourcing specialist, neither situation is one you want to face. Take all the steps you can to minimize the possibility that you will ever have to.

Watch your business relationship size like a hawk. Ask your key partners directly what percentage your business represents for them. Ask about other customers and their impact. Even if your company is correctly aligned so as not to be exposed unnecessarily, you face the same risks when another customer exerts an exceptional influence. It is imperative that you know the sizes of their top five accounts, and be very cautious when any of them exceed the above limits. The risks of inattention are too great.

Don't overlook the value of face-to-face factory visits with key suppliers. A surprising amount of knowledge is available for the harvesting by a set of sharp eyes and keen hearing, as we've already seen.

The first thing is to insist on visiting the supplier's factory. Don't waste your time visiting the sales office, where you can be wined, dined, and fed the company pabulum, yet learn very little of what you must know. The factory is where the story is. You must invest the shoe leather to walk the floor end-to-end, to learn about your products, the manufacturing processes required to make it, and how the vendor does what it does that makes it unique.

If It Looks Like a Duck, and Walks Like a Duck . . .

Begin with overall impressions. Contrary to common knowledge, first impressions can be the most insightful, especially when based on instincts built on past experience.

Is the facility clean and neat, appearing well organized? Are materials kept together in orderly groupings? Are the machines and the floor kept clean? What is the general appearance of the employees? A factory that appears neat, orderly, and well organized, probably is. Employees in clean uniforms, self-pride evident in their personage, will care about their work, and ultimately, your product.

A good example regarding appearances and first impressions concerns a Midwest drive motor manufacturer I visited a few years ago. Its product began with a casting, and progressed through several machining steps on heavy turning centers. The process required lots of lubrication and cutting oils, and it created a considerable amount of metal shavings at the lathes.

In touring the facility, two things struck me. The first was that all employees wore company shirts, even machine tool operators and cleanup personnel. I asked our guide about this, who explained that policy dictated that every employee must wear a company shirt, and noted that the employees paid half the cost. They had a personal investment in their appearance.

Each operator ran two or more machines, and constantly loaded and unloaded in-process parts. Yet to a person, their work clothes were clean and neat, their work areas strictly organized, and all scrap metal under control and mechanically removed almost from the moment it was generated.

The other point was how spotless the floor was, beyond anything I might have expected in a factory. It was completely tiled, not the more common sealed concrete normally found in a factory setting. There were no spots of grease, no pools of oil or standing water, and not a single, aged black stain to be found.

A purely coincidental event illustrated my point. While watching a particular cutting machine, the rubber cooling oil line burst, spewing cutting oil in every direction. The subsequent employee actions would have made any well-trained emergency team proud.

The operator immediately shut down his machine and turned off the source of spewing oil. Once he was sure the machine was secure, he called the spill team in. Several members of the team arrived within seconds. They contained the spill by surrounding it with portable dams. While one group began vacuuming the liquids, another team began wiping down adjacent machines that had gotten sprayed, and then thoroughly cleaned the machine that had broken. A third maintenance team was at work replacing the damaged hose.

Within a few minutes the floor had been cleaned, all machines had been wiped down, the defective hose replaced, and, with everyone's careful oversight, the manufacturing process was carefully restarted, verifying that everything worked correctly.

If a company takes that much care in its process and facility, it is reasonable to believe that it will take a great deal of pride and interest in its products, and would make my job as buyer easier in the process.

Another aspect in learning about a company is to observe how it manages its inventory. If parts are scattered all about, the company may have too much cash invested in inventory, unnecessarily inflating its cost of doing business and, thus, the prices charged to you. These conditions also lead to higher probabilities of surprise stockouts leading to disruptions in your supply chain.

Note who the vendor's suppliers are. Do you know anything about these companies? Find out about them—their skills, locations, and means of doing business. Don't overlook the Internet as a valuable resource of information once you return to your hotel or office.

A regular visit to a supplier sends the message that you are interested in the company and how it conducts its business. In touring the facility, check out all process steps required. Make it clear that you want to learn what it takes to make your product. You will be trying to spot any weaknesses, and finding ideas for improvement. Before you leave, you should have a good understanding of the major concepts of a critical supplier's business.

Get to Know the Person Behind the Voice

The last point I want to make is the most important. It is much easier to do business with someone you know, and who knows you. Aren't we all more comfortable being able to put a face with a voice on the other end of the line, or the name on the bottom of a letter or e-mail message?

Visit each other's offices; get to know not only the person, but also the environment in which she works. Notice things about the person's work space, how she keeps personal effects, mementos that indicate what she values, and books on the shelf. You will be surprised at how often you will find something that you have in common, either inside or outside the work situation. You might discover a mutual passion for baseball, or a keen interest in photography, or places that you've visited in your personal travels. Every time you can connect on an additional level, it is another reinforcement in cementing a strong business relationship.

One last word of warning: This book talks often about the advantages of technology in doing business today, and extols the benefits to be derived from an efficient electronic business medium. Be constantly on guard, however, that the medium does not become a faceless, nonemotional means of conducting business, and, in the name of efficiency, suck all the humanity out of your daily contacts.

"Technology is, in fact, the greatest enabler of our day. But if we're not careful, we can also become *dis*-abled by technology." R. David Nelson, a member of the ISM board of directors, goes on to say, "While technology provides us with many helpful tools, those tools are a poor substitute for relationships—the basis of every long-term business success."[2]

Think carefully about what Nelson says, and take it to heart. It could one day mean the difference between success and failure in your career.

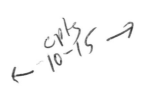

Summary

It was common in history for company owners to do business only with people they knew and trusted. It was important to know the man before you sent him money, an old adage went.

With the advent of faster communications and the shrinking of the business world, time replaced personal knowledge, and we are currently witnessing an explosion in the arena of technological communication capabilities. With it, we are losing the edge in personally knowing who we do business with.

Good business practices dictate that we thoroughly understand our products and markets, along with our suppliers and their capabilities. The knowledge requirement extends beyond the product, to the company and the businessperson we are to work with.

Notes

1. "Purchasing Managers, Buyers, and Purchasing Agents," Bureau of Labor Statistics, U.S. Department of Labor, *Occupational Outlook Handbook*, www.bls.gov/oco/ocos023.htm.
2. R. David Nelson, "Putting a Face on Business," *Inside Supply Management*, Institute for Supply Management (July 2002), p. 4.

CHAPTER 10

Do What You Do Best, Outsource the Rest

FOR MANY YEARS, the directive of American capitalism was to vertically integrate. The assumption was that the more steps in the process that a company directly controlled, the more efficiently the company would operate. Continuous profit improvements were the expected end result.

An example might be a heavy equipment manufacturer, such as Caterpillar or John Deere. These manufacturers owned their own foundries, making castings for engines and heavy parts. They managed their machine shops, believing this was the only way to adequately control the process and quality of the parts. All welding was done in-house, as well as final assembly, including subassemblies like pumps, valves, and cylinders. They even manufactured their own high-pressure hoses. They owned the paint facilities, manufactured their decals, and printed catalogs and service manuals.

Vertical integration was the perceived key to success, and was the basis for a lot of capital spending over the years. But was it the right thing to do?

75

Beware False Efficiencies

With few exceptions, most companies cannot adequately utilize the resources invested in the equipment, facilities, and staffs to justify the processes owned. Often, the return on analysis equation used by the financial types to measure the performance of each dollar invested only makes sense with full utilization of the resources. In other words, they may own the biggest piece of equipment, but then have to run it at full tilt in order for it to make financial sense.

But what about actual demand?

As a sourcing specialist, a strong sense of skepticism in the make-inside-versus-outsource discussion will serve you well. Assumed in-house efficiencies are another notorious instance where common sense and logic can direct you down the wrong path.

I recall a case study from several years ago about a large company that had suffered the indignity of being passed around to a succession of owners.[1,2] It never quite seemed to fit into any one company's long-term plans, and although it had a strong brand name and certain customer cachet, it remained a financial underperformer.

A team of managers within the company decided they could do a better job of running the company, and they bought Harley-Davidson Motor Company from AMF.

The facility was noted for having some of the most sophisticated tooling and machinery in the industry. Multimillion-dollar turning and stamping centers put out hundreds or thousands of parts per hour, efficiently and effortlessly. Automated conveyers served the large factory, with hanging chain drives whisking loads of parts and assemblies along their way to another work center.

Yet, even with all this sophisticated equipment and automation, the production line always seemed to be stopped for a lack of parts. The open areas around the facility were filled with partially completed machines, all awaiting critical shortages of one kind or another. The product issues didn't end once a motorcycle was completed. Overall quality was poor, and it was a common joke that when a customer bought one of these units, he should also invest in an oil company because the machines leaked so much.

When the new owners looked over their facility, they wisely decided it was time to stop and really look at everything, reevaluate all assumptions behind their process, and, most important, take stock of what parts they had and what they needed.

It was obvious there was a complete mismatch of parts required to parts available. In some cases, they discovered a year's supply of an item like a specialized gas tank hanging on the sophisticated conveyor hooks, while they couldn't find something like a fender in the place.

Management found instances where the only way some very expensive machinery could pay for itself was to run constantly. The financial efficiency numbers looked great, because each part was manufactured at a very low cost. Unfortunately, actual demand came nowhere close to matching the output capabilities of the equipment. Supply far outstripped demand, wasting money and pulling resources away from other parts that were actually required.

The lesson illustrated here is to look beyond the numbers when working toward a sourcing decision. What Harley-Davidson accomplished over time was to replace the multimillion-dollar machinery with less efficient but much lower-cost equipment. They were able to build exactly what they needed, then change over the tooling to build the next part required. In this manner they reduced costs significantly, while at the same time reducing inventory levels. The company built fewer parts, but more motorcycles.

Another example was with Ampex Corporation, which I referred to in Chapter 3. Its midwestern factory included a very large metal shop with the latest in sophisticated machine tools.

The plant manager actively solicited business for his shop from the six other divisions of the corporation, making the case for keeping the work inside the company versus outsourcing it.

I was part of a corporate-level team doing an evaluation of the facility relative to offshore or other, local procurement. My plan was to establish equal quality performance levels, and then do a strict cost analysis and comparison, recommending the least total cost of acquisition alternative, including freight and volume cost savings.

The very first surprise was that, for comparison purposes, the fixed overhead portions of the internal costs were to be excluded from the comparison, but included on the external side.

Fixed overhead is the cost of the building, floor space, property taxes, insurance, and basic heat and light, among others. These are expenses not directly related to producing product, and they must be paid whether the facility is running or empty.

The logic for this erroneous assumption was that the building and machinery were there anyway, so those costs were not related to the cost of production. Many companies at the time used the same thought process in their decision making.

Fixed overhead is a significant portion of the costs of any product, and when removed from the equation, makes the decision appear easy; everything will be done inside. An outsider's price included fixed overhead, and thus could never adequately compete with the internal costs.

For a period of time, an ever-increasing level of companywide production requirements was moved to this facility. The volume would have grown endlessly except for other obstacles to success, such as exceeding capacity and not meeting schedules.

The financial model used in the decision-making process suggested that it was always cheaper to produce product internally. Thus, a case could be made that more items should come into the facility, and the facility would have to continue growing and adding capacity, drawing even more product into the operation, spending more unreported fixed overhead dollars, and so on, and so on. This could continue right up to the point when the doors would be shuttered because there were no profits, and all the money had been spent. All because the decision-making assumptions depended upon false efficiencies.

Find the Best Solution

The collective thinking was that, since the cost was already sunk, it was best to absorb the excess capacity. The managers assumed that as long as the variable costs, such as direct labor and materials, were being covered, then the company was making money.

This in itself is a workable, though not ideal, plan. But once the absorption numbers began to improve, then management erroneously assumed efficiencies were also improving, and they started looking for more work. In other words, additional and subsequent bad decisions were made to justify an initial bad decision.

Whenever excess capacity is on line and cannot reasonably be consumed, the correct focus has to be to get rid of it. Two bad decisions never equal one good one.

Today, outsourcing is becoming more widely accepted, and a

sourcing specialist needs to understand the process. A wise company considering outsourcing will undertake a serious study to honestly learn where the company strengths lie, and then move toward outsourcing the rest of its requirements.

Outsourcing began in earnest in the electronics industry during the early 1980s. Small companies sprang up, such as Solectron in San Jose, which specialized in the processes required to assemble printed circuit boards and wiring harnesses. Early users of these companies saw them merely as a temporary addition to capacity, to be used when peak demands exceeded current ability to produce. Customers supplied complete kits of materials and assembly drawings, and the suppliers were little more than board-stuffing houses. As soon as the demand subsided, the work would be pulled quickly back inside.

Gradually the subcontracting companies grew, and their skill sets improved. One of the first process changes was when customers began ordering turnkey products for the complete assembly. In most cases, the subcontractor supplied all of the components in addition to final assembly labor.

These processes continued to grow, and the suppliers began building and testing completed assemblies to a forecast. Gradually they took over module work, and ordered, built, and tested complete, multilevel assemblies.

Today companies like Solectron are multinational in strength. They not only offer assembly and test sites around the world, but in some cases, their own facilities manufacture many of the raw components. Vertical integration has moved from the final consumer to the outsourcing supplier.

In 1995, Ford Motor Company undertook a review process, called Ford 2000, and came to a few interesting conclusions. In order to assure its future growth and success, it acknowledged that it had a great team of engineers and visionaries capable of designing the automobiles of the future. It felt comfortable that it had the right studios and processes to encourage freethinking and new ideas.

Ford also felt that it had a very strong assembly capability, with modern plants equipped with the latest in machine tools, robots, and efficient processes. Assembly costs were the second-largest expense, behind materials, and Ford believed it had the resources and skills required to efficiently build Ford automobiles.

What management also concluded (and it ended up a leader in

the industry by making this decision) was that its core weakness lay in manufacturing parts and subassemblies. It realized that, instead of trying to compete with suppliers better able to make these items, it would be a wiser strategic move to create alliances with quality suppliers that were capable of meeting Ford's needs for parts and assemblies, on a JIT basis.[3]

To date, Ford has invested billions of dollars into this program. The results confirm the wisdom of the program. Product lead time has been reduced from over sixty days to less than fifteen. Communications within the company have improved, the amount of common parts and designs across all model lines has increased significantly, and the number of critical vendors has been reduced from over 1,000 to less than fifty.

Deciding to Outsource

The outsourcing decision can be simplified into a two-thought process.

The first is to determine what it is your company does best. In the Ford example, it knew that it designed and assembled automobiles better than anyone else. This was the company's core competency.

The second step is to make the decision to outsource the rest. Once misplaced pride and the "not invented here" (NIH) syndrome is pushed out of the equation, it becomes easier to make the right decision. There are certain processes that your suppliers are expert in. They do the work all day, every day, and chances are they have probably forgotten more about the process than your company can ever hope to learn. The lesson then is to build upon this resource, utilize the suppliers' expertise, and let them make your parts. By choosing the right supplier, you will assure yourself the right part, at the right time, at the right price.

Another benefit to outsourcing is that it frees up company resources to pursue other, more directly beneficial investments in your organization's future. By selling off the expensive machine tools, vacating the large factory buildings, reducing the staff and overhead to support these less-than-efficient investments, capital and labor are made available to focus on your core competencies.

Economies of Scale

Another reason to outsource is for the economies of scale achieved by potential suppliers, contributing further to your total cost reduction goals.

Let's take a hypothetical example in the Ford Motor case and see where it leads.

Computer-numeric-controlled turning centers are getting more sophisticated each year. Multimillion-dollar machines are capable of loading a hundred tools or more at a time, and they can handle part-mounting fixtures of several tons in weight. These mounts can be designed to load many different, nonrelated parts at one time. With a programmed twist of the mount and an automatic change of the tool, an entirely different part can be made moments after its predecessor. Automated loading and unloading lines are mated to the centers, further promoting efficiency and cost reduction.

These benefits might not accrue to Ford, for example, because if it had this equipment on its own, it could not completely or efficiently utilize it. In other words, downtime would be experienced when different parts are needed from other centers.

This is not the case for the CNC turning center company. On the same mount and even possibly in the next slot, a Chevrolet part can be set up and ready to run once the Ford part is complete. The normally scheduled empty times are being filled by other parts for other customers, thereby reducing total costs for both customers. The CNC turning company makes parts all day, every day, and learns new efficiencies and cost reductions in the process.

Do Your Homework

In the early 1980s, Japanese manufacturing companies were ridiculing the American investment in high-cost, long-run machining centers and automated manufacturing lines. This was a bit of an anomaly, since its industrial companies were noted suppliers of the complicated, high-precision equipment used in the United States. Where we were making large runs in order to justify the price of the machining centers, Japan was making high-precision pieces of equipment using older, simpler machines, set up to run exactly the number of parts required, and then turned off. Its industrial focus was to spend the resources not in the equipment, but in the tooling. Japan's industrial conclusion was that the financial return was in quick-turn tooling, not expensive machining centers.

Another area for the sourcing specialist to examine is the number of customers who purchase the same, or similar, parts from your outsourcing candidate. A shop that is already busy making similar products for others is often significantly down the learning curve and able to provide cost and efficiency benefits far outweighing a new, in-house start-up shop.

Outsourcing can also help mitigate the risk inherent in a new product or design. Initial forecasts might be low, and the long-term forecast not solidified. Before investing in the required infrastructure to take on producing the new product in-house, the learning curve might get started with an outsourcing process. This is particularly true in cases where an investment in machine tools is required. A case can easily be made for renting the required equipment until plans are solidified.

Microsoft has been working closely with Flextronics on the outsourcing of its XBox product.[4] In initially developing the relationship, it was looking for a partner that had a global sourcing presence and a wide array of OEM work experience.

In transferring the production responsibility, Microsoft looked carefully at how Flextronics managed inventory control, new technology, and relationships with its suppliers. One selling point was that Flextronics had set up relationships with key vendors to look directly into Flextronics forecasts, allowing suppliers to react quickly to changes in demand.

Another area of interest to Microsoft was the specific part capability of Flextronics in terms of ordering, pricing, and quality control. Each part required was carefully reviewed for contract and sourcing strengths, with the result that several key components were kept under the control of Microsoft's engineering and quality departments. This varied from parts procured off contracts maintained by Microsoft all the way to its supplying the required parts to Flextronics. Microsoft maintained control over its strategic suppliers involved with its outsourcing suppliers.

Summary

The globalization of the customer and supplier base is forcing companies to become much more efficient and cost driven than ever before.

The signs are everywhere. Brand-name cache is being reduced every day. Consumers flock to low-cost department stores and outlets, where price is far more important than name.

Air travel is little more than a packed bus going 550 miles per hour in the sky, with customers wedged in like sardines in a tin. As much as we all complain about these conditions, at the end of a trip we don't brag about the quality of the food or the extra space afforded to us by an unusual airline. Instead, the topic of conversation around the dinner table is who got the lowest fare on the Internet. The airlines are merely serving the customers' real demands.

Price and quality are the drivers today. In order to achieve the constantly growing demand for the two, suppliers at all levels must be vigilant for opportunities to improve efficiencies and reduce cost. Outsourcing is a key player in this arena.

Once a company does the analysis to determine its core competencies, the message is clear that the next logical step is to look for a skilled, qualified outsourcing partner. "Keep the best and outsource the rest" will become the new road map to success.

As part of the implementation team, the sourcing specialist must know how to look for the best supplier, know what to look for in candidates, and understand what it will take to get the program under way.

Notes

1. Rich Teerlink and Lee Ozley, *More Than a Motorcycle: The Leadership Journey at Harley-Davidson* (Boston: Harvard Business School Press, 2000).
2. Peter C. Reid, *Well Made in America: Lessons from Harley-Davidson on Being the Best* (New York: McGraw-Hill, 1991).
3. Robert D. Austin, "Ford Motor Company: Supply Chain Strategy," Harvard Business School, Case Study 9-699-198, Rev. (December 2001); Betty A. Marton, "If It Ain't Broke, Fix It Anyway: Communicating to Create Change at Ford," Harvard Management Communication Letter (May 1999).
4. Jim Carbone, "Outsourcing the XBox," *Purchasing* (August 15, 2002), www.purchasing.com.

CHAPTER 11

JIT, Kan Ban, SMED, and Other Funny Names

JUST-IN-TIME (JIT) has been a part of the American business land-scape for over thirty years. Sadly, it has taken that long to learn how to use it. As you read in the previous chapter, the Ford 2000 program documents the significant investment made by the automobile giant in changing how it will do business in the future, and the role that JIT plays in its planned success.

It might be interesting to create a listing of all the funny names, acronyms, projects, buzzwords, and shorthand initials that industry has gone through over the years, all in search of the perfect solution, the one-size-fits-all answer to every business question.

A quick mental survey brings to mind managing by objectives, quality circles, zero defects, total quality control, matrix management, quality is free, ISO, CE, and Focus Forecasting, among others. One of the latest feel-good buzzwords is partnership, a topic addressed further in Chapter 19.

Many of the best minds in industry and academia have searched for that elusive formula, the one calculation that would improve forecast accuracy and remove the mathematical equivalent of uncertainty.

Judging by the recent crop of business books and press, this goal has quietly been put to rest in the graveyard of unlikely ideas, to lie in eternal peace.

Just as there is no universal formula for forecasting, so is there no one perfect manufacturing tool or technique capable of addressing all the industrial variables that might affect business performance. However, there are some techniques that, correctly applied, have been successful for a number of years, and are flexible enough to have a variety of applications. I discuss three of them in this chapter. Unlike many of the techniques and buzzwords of the past, properly installed, JIT, Kan Ban, and SMED work.

In general, JIT, Kan Ban, and SMED were up and running successfully in Japan when most American companies couldn't spell them. Manufacturing companies that successfully implemented these techniques achieved quality improvements that are now legendary, and they forced a rapid change in the way American companies faced up to the growing expectations demanded by customers who were suddenly offered products that performed to their expectations.

Just-in-Time

Like many of the most effective techniques in business, JIT is deceptively simple in its proper application. It is an inventory scheduling process that limits the delivery of raw materials to just before the items are required, or just-in-time delivery.

A clear illustration of JIT is set in Japan in the late 1970s. Automobile manufacturers were the first to successfully implement JIT. Factories featured a long assembly line, with small quantities of material staged at each workstation, awaiting installation as the car moved along the line. Prior to the beginning of the first shift in the morning, there would be no material in the factory, and nothing in process on the assembly line.

As each day began, workers arrived in sequence as partial assemblies were conveyed to their particular workstation. Material and parts were delivered in the same manner, on a staggered, sequential schedule, progressively down the assembly line, minutes before their actual need, or just in time. This process continued through the completion of the last car at the end of the second shift. When the line began to close down, work stopped in the same order. Parts delivery would end, and people left work for the day as the last car assembly moved out of their workstation, on to the next one in line. At the end of the second shift, when the final car rolled off the assembly line, there were no raw materials left in the factory, no partially completed cars, and no material at risk of obsolescence or loss. The inventory level in the company at the end of the workday was zero.

The benefits of a properly run JIT program are significant. As the consuming company, there is a minimal level of inventory investment, freeing up capital for other uses. The risk of quality issues is lowered, because the volume of potentially defective parts in-house is low. Fixes can be done quickly and easily. Because there are no parts collecting dust on warehouse shelves, handling is reduced; there is no need for a warehouse at all, which frees up dead space for more efficient utilization. Finally, inventory accuracy improves significantly, because there is less on hand at any given time, and count discrepancies quickly become apparent and are easier to address and correct.

The Fallacy of JIT in the United States

JIT is only now beginning to be broadly understood and correctly implemented by American industry, thirty years after becoming a cornerstone of success in Japan.

JIT is not a means of forcing your suppliers to invest heavily in your inventory requirements, where the only real achievement is moving the stockroom from your facility to the vendor's. Under this process, companies still pay for the high levels of inventory investment required, only in the form of a higher price instead of direct material investment.

JIT can only succeed when you openly and honestly share your business information with suppliers, so they can accurately gauge the amount of business to expect from you. This is not the place for exaggerated forecasts in the hopes of obtaining a better price, nor for an overestimation of the business levels expected from your customers. If you have 50 percent of your customer's business, don't forecast its total demand as coming to your company. If there is a general economic recession in the country, don't forecast as though there is an expansion.

The next step in the JIT process, and the one missing in the American model, is to work with and encourage the vendors you wish to participate in this program to actively share this same information with their suppliers, with the same goals in mind. By divulging the committed portion of its business, your vendor should be able to work with its suppliers to institute the same forecast commitment for raw materials and finished products. True JIT achieves its success only when the process is run completely back up the supply chain, obtaining understanding and working agreements every step along the way.

Kan Ban

Kan Ban is a simple technique that will aid in improving performance results at an organization with an absolute minimal investment in time, effort, or capital. Its possible applications are almost limitless, including uses in raw material, production processes, storeroom control, and vendor-managed inventory. We will focus on just two applications useful from the sourcing specialist's point of view.

In the automobile-manufacturing example used above, the supplier delivered its materials directly to the consuming workstation on the manufacturing floor. There was a specific location, often a marked or painted spot on the floor. This is referred to as a Kan Ban square. The idea was that the square could be filled at any time, but material could never be delivered that would be in excess of that allowed by the confines of the Kan Ban square. The rate of consumption, length of time it took to restock, frequency of delivery, production, case lot size, and physical size determined the amount of material allowed within the confines of the square. The square was always to be as small as possible. Kan Ban worked with JIT to correctly schedule replenishments, while controlling on-hand inventory.

The second application is a bit different. In this case, the sourcing specialist finalizes an agreement with a critical supplier, covering specific products used in her facility. The volumes, prices, deliveries, packaging requirements, and specifications, for instance, are also agreed to as part of the negotiations. Once the terms have been finalized, the actual control of the schedule is then turned over to the material or production control function for day-to-day releases.

The result is that, once the available material shrinks to a predetermined point, such as opening the last Kan Ban square, or a minimal box of the part, the Kan Ban card is forwarded to the material planners to release the next shipment from the vendor. A blanket order would be in place, and each delivery directed by the material planner would go against the master order. In this manner, sourcing is freed of the repetitive task of placing purchase orders for the same product under the same or very similar circumstances.

Adequately trained production control staff or manufacturing line personnel can serve the material planner function just as well. This process is also a natural for locally controlled, vendor-managed inventory.

Single Minute Exchange of Die (SMED)

Although not as popular or widely understood as JIT or Kan Ban, single minute exchange of die (SMED) is a technique identified and exploited by Japanese manufacturers that made a significant contribution toward their successes in reducing inventory.

American industry has a tendency to think big and sophisticated when it comes to machine tools. Past practices dictated the purchase of highly automated equipment capable of turning out thousands of pieces per hour, at a very low per-piece cost. When run constantly, the difference in efficiency and costs compared to lesser equipment can be staggering.

Too often, actual performance has shown that the output of these machines far exceeded total demand. Warehouses, overhead chains, and factory floors are regularly buried in parts efficiently produced, just not needed. The machines are kept running to support the false financial numbers used to justify the initial investment. This was clearly illustrated earlier with Harley-Davidson.

JIT and Kan Ban worked successfully in the Far East for two reasons. The first was that the decision to run (or not run) a particular piece of equipment was driven by true demand for the resulting part, not by an accounting number. Equipment ran when parts were required, and it was turned off when they were not. The amount of actual machine running time was of no concern in the decision-making process.

The second reason was that machine-tooling choices were based on process flexibility, not output-per-minute. In other words, a machine tool that had a multitude of capabilities was deemed more desirable than a machine with faster output of more specialized parts. This is where SMED plays an important role.

SMED drives the practice that flexibility and speed of tool change-over is more important than output-per-time period. If a factory can change the tooling with relative ease, it can make more parts, of a wider variety, than a machine that takes hours or even days to change tooling. With SMED, the minimal number of actual required parts can be run, the machine stopped, the tooling changed, and the machine up and running again in short order, making the next few parts needed in the process. This changing of tooling continues all during the manufacturing day, making small runs of several items, instead of huge runs of several days or weeks' worth of production, which then sits around awaiting demand.

Smaller, less specialized, more flexible equipment is much more desirable than larger, dedicated, and specialized machining centers. The true cost is recognized as the run time and resulting inventory investment, not in the tooling investment.

Summary

JIT and Kan Ban are widely misunderstood techniques that have been abused by many companies. They often have been held out to suppliers as a carrot during good times, a stick during bad times. That was never the original intent, and will never be a measure of success over the long term. The limited vision of past purchasing functions saw both processes as a system that forced suppliers to invest heavily in warehousing and inventory, just in case the buyer needed it. The fallacy was that this was a cost-reduction measure, when, in fact, all it did was move the costs from inventory investment to purchase price.

SMED is not something easily controlled by sourcing, but it is a technique that must be understood. It is a strong tool in the cost-reduction equation, one that can be discussed not only with your own company, but also with suppliers and vendors as an aid in training them to become more efficient.

As an effective sourcing specialist, it is imperative that you thoroughly understand JIT, Kan Ban, and SMED, and train your vendors to ensure that they understand them. By working together, you will discover many applications for all three techniques in your growing partnership. By mutually attaining the successes inherent in each one, you will strengthen the opportunities for significant returns for both parties.

Learning to Harness the Tools of Technology

TWENTY YEARS OF MY CAREER were invested in various aspects of the technology industry. I've been fortunate to have been involved with leading-edge products in disk drives, add-on memory modules, large-scale thermal printers, scientific analytical instruments, audio-video broadcast equipment for the television industry, Winchester disk platters, core memory for the defense industry, and high-performance computers.

A key to success in the technology industry is being the first to market with a product that has a perceived leap in features over the competition. Most such items I was associated with during those years were state-of-the-art designs, melding known products with leading-edge components, pushing the boundaries of accepted performance.

From the sourcing standpoint, the success of a new product often hinged on a critical element, supplied by a sole-source small company or start-up, whose technology was the key to the future success of the new techno-tool.

Computing Power, the Early Years

During my career, I witnessed the growth of the first personal computers for business applications. The PC (personal computer), as it became known, ran on the DOS operating system from a small software company in Redmond, Washington. In those days the significant competitor was an operating system called CPM. Legends abound about how the market migrated to DOS, to the point where today it's likely impossible to separate fact from bigger-than-life company lore.

Apple Computer, generally acknowledged as the leader in creativity and ease of use, was a fascinating study. The group of jeans-and-sweatshirt-clad, longhaired, radical workers in Cupertino were considered to be over the edge, even by California standards. They were fanatical when it came to Apple, believed in themselves, and held a universal contempt for the competition. Every new idea was incredibly awesome and the path below their Nikes or Reeboks led to a future exclusively theirs—a string of ever-higher peaks of success as far as the imagination could see.

As happens when a company mistakes its own PR for gospel, Apple continued to look inward, ever ready to tell customers what they should want, and preaching how lucky they were to be able to get it from Apple. Introspection is good for the soul, but intelligence obtained by looking in a mirror prevented Steve Jobs and John Scully from noticing that customers were slipping away. While the gurus continued patting themselves on the back, that small company in Redmond grew into a thousand-pound gorilla called Microsoft, and the cumbersome PC became the de facto industry standard.

History contains countless examples of similar forces in effect across a spectrum of industries, including automobiles, steel, airlines, and shoes. There is a lesson to be learned by serious sourcing specialists.

Universal Lessons for Sourcing

Watch for suppliers who behave in this manner. If they are arrogant or confident beyond reason in their product, market, and customer understanding, or believe they are the only ones out there capable of doing what they do, be cautious. Chances are they are heading for a fall. Take steps to ensure that you don't trip on the carcass and topple over right along with them.

Be ever-vigilant for new ideas, products, and processes as they pertain to your company. No matter how remote the possible relationship, if something piques your sourcing interest and instincts, there often is a reason for it.

The original total worldwide market for mainframe computers was estimated to be no larger than a handful of users at most. IBM, by selling millions of mainframes beginning with the models 360 and 370, proved those forecasts wrong.

In the ensuing years, the demand for personal computers was believed to exist strictly in the minds of geeky engineering and egghead types, too far out there creatively to drive a large demand in the general population. Sound familiar?

Subsequent to its success with mainframes, IBM severely underestimated this market, and in a desperate catch-up mode, underserved it with overpriced, inferior products sold to a market it perceived would be satisfied on the basis of three blue letters on the front of the case.

The nimble company that attacked, and for decades owned, the mainframe business evolved into a behemoth looking inward. It never saw the rise of the PC market, which, when networked together, easily replaced its mainframe business in many applications.

E-Commerce

All this leads to a discussion of the Internet and e-commerce, sometimes known as B2B, or business to business.

For the companies addressed in this book, sourcing personnel should consider e-commerce as anything having to do with an electronic means of doing business. This ranges from simple Web research to ordering, processing, and paying for goods under an electronic, paperless umbrella.

To paraphrase a popular marketing euphemism, to date, B2B has sold lots of sizzle, but delivered very little steak. The concept is brilliant, the technology rapidly catching up with the need, the hype much greater than the execution, the perceived value not yet clear or widely understood. Initial concepts were poorly thought out, the details not planned for, and the amount of investment and discipline required severely underestimated. It is a case of the concept far out-stripping the resources.

None of this is to be taken as a failure of the e-commerce or the Internet, nor is it an unworkable idea, just one with the kinks still to be worked out. As noted in *BusinessWeek,* "The Internet and network business model already are the common sense of businesses, even if not all companies yet choose or know how to apply it."[1]

Finding sources for products these days is much more efficient because of the electronic tools at our disposal. The old days of thumbing through the Thomas Register, working the yellow pages, or calling current suppliers looking for new ones have been supplanted by the Internet and other tools that improve efficiency. Company Web sites or complete catalogs on a CD, stored near your PC and conveniently at your disposal, are tools that make research faster, focused, and efficient.

In learning all you can about a company you are considering as a possible source for your materials, there is nothing like a Web site as a vast resource of information. Depending upon its level of sophistication, you often can discover key contacts within the company, items they consider their most important products, pricing and lead time information, names, addresses, and phone numbers. You can even learn of their e-business capabilities.

Another effective use is searching out their competitors, as well as information on companies that might use their product. This gives you a line on references, as well as possible other sources.

While we are on the topic of research, don't overlook another use of the Internet. It is an ideal tool for helping to identify who your competitors might be. What are the key aspects of their current markets, as indicated by the products emphasized on their Web site? What is their pricing matrix compared to yours? Who are their key contacts? How do you contact them? Are they ahead of you in the technology game, vis-à-vis B2B?

Effective search engines, such as Yahoo!, Netscape, MSN, Lycos, or my favorite, Google, have made Web searching an easy task. Just type in a topic or name to find a host of possible sites for what you are seeking. In the span of a few mouse clicks, you can be at a company site and garnering critical information that you would have spent hours, or days, searching for only a few years ago. And the engines are getting better each day at organizing and sorting the over

900 million Web sites currently operating, able to quickly match the request with the likely correct site.

There are formal B2B companies that also serve this market, and Ariba is considered the largest online transaction supplier by many companies today. It offers what it refers to as a spend management process to allow companies to transact business and exchange documents through its network.[2]

There are many other suppliers of B2B and auction-site software. I have listed a few of them in the References section of this book under "Outsourcing Companies, Programs, and Software."

As a buyer keying into the more sophisticated supplier sites, you will electronically place your order directly to its order desk, or in more advanced companies, right to its shipping department. Here your order will be verified online, the inventory availability will be determined and allocated, the product picked, packaged, and shipped, the best routing determined, and a shipping notice and invoice created and e-mailed back to you. All of this is done in minutes, without personal communication or paper exchanging hands.

Since most procurement departments are paying for IS support, it makes sense to utilize the resource in the most efficient manner. As a sourcing specialist always on the lookout to improve processes and procedures, and with a constant eye out to reduce total costs, you should carefully look into the opportunities of placing as many orders as possible electronically. Significant cost reductions can be realized, along with increased efficiencies, by placing orders directly to your suppliers with no paper being printed, handled, mailed, or filed.

Chapter 13 documents how smaller, yet nimble companies can compete with the General Motorses of the world when it comes to sourcing strategies. Unfortunately, as you dig deeper into the electronic world of sourcing, you will find many strategies not economical or even available to you, as a smaller company. There are ways to compete, however, as the chapter will demonstrate.

Terminology and Techniques

All of this does not mean the small business should not be aware of some of the techniques and understand some of the terminology in the electronic world of sourcing.

For example, you will run across auction sites. The most effective of these, reverse auctions, will put out to bid a certain amount of business, with possible suppliers bidding on all or a part of the business. Let's say, for example, that a large retailer puts out on a site that it is interested in purchasing a million bathroom scatter rugs over the course of a year. As part of the reverse auction, it might specify the colors, the minimal acceptable quality level, the expected delivery lot size, the number of locations to be supported, and the payment terms. It will then invite suppliers to participate in the auction for its business, with a definite time and date for the close of the auction.

The goal is to have several possible suppliers bidding for the business, all using the same specifications, assumptions, and time pressure to finalize the process. From the buyer's standpoint, at auction close, it knows exactly what to expect in quality, terms and conditions, and price.

Another term garnering a great deal of attention today is EDI, electronic data interface. What is commonly meant here is the ability for the orders, as suggested above, to be directly placed, and their status ascertained, either through a Web site or some other means of electronic communication.

Several large retail chains have already taken a quantum leap ahead in this process, by linking their POS data directly to their supplier sites. In this manner, it is theoretically possible for the replenishment order to be placed with the supplier at the moment the perpetual inventory has dropped below its order point, as directed by the POS data at the checkout scanner. Thus, at the moment of sale, the replacement order is automatically flashed to the supplier's shipping dock, triggering a shipper, pulling and kitting from inventory, scheduling for a freight pickup, and flashing back to the retailer all the relevant shipping details. All this is done in an electronic wink of an eye.

But even this fantastic leap in technology is rapidly becoming old news. The EDI link just described is focused from the final vendor to the customer sight. In other words, it is focused from your company to your customer's site.

What if, as the creative sourcing specialist you are, you think this process through and ask why not send that same data through you and move it directly to your suppliers? Therefore, when you receive the order from the retailer, if it draws your inventory below an order point, your vendor is directly triggered into action. Think of using the same process of sharing your POS data with your suppliers, with the expected same result.

Source of Demand

Most direct material purchases for a manufacturing company are made based upon a computer customer order and forecasting process, such as MRP II or ERP.

These processes convert a forecast or customer order for end products into a detailed requirements plan of individual components and assemblies required to make that order. At the buyer level, this means a planning tool to create requirements for parts orders you need to place.

Another step forward in the e-commerce arena is allowing key suppliers directly into these MRP screens. This technique allows the supplier to look directly at all requirements having to do with parts (or product) it supplies to your company. These screens contain your current on-hand inventory positions. They also show planned deliveries already in place with the vendor, order positions, and future forecasts. Depending upon the planning horizon used by your company, a vendor will also see the long-term demand for its product.

The two-fold benefit here is that your supplier can effectively use this data as a tool to ensure that it plans correctly for your current and future demands, while using the data in working with its key suppliers to assure a continued, adequate supply of material required by your company. It can also effectively use the information when negotiating for future business and possible price, or other concessions, from its vendors.

This has been experimented with for several years now, but it is not yet widely used in industry. The day will come when it must be.

Properly installed, electronic planning systems allow product to appear at your receiving dock or floor location at the proper time, and, in the right quantity, all this is accomplished without pieces of unwieldy paper exchanging hands or touch-tone tag played on the phone lines.

Efficiency Improvements

The time it takes to do the processing of almost any of the e-commerce techniques listed here, or those that are only dreams to come, is microseconds, at worst. With the proper front-end preparations and safeguards, we reduce a cumbersome, time-consuming, and expensive order process to the level of a few keystrokes at worst, no human intervention, at best. The cost-saving potential is enormous.

To put this in scale, e-procurement covers 95 percent of what mega-giant IBM Corporation does in annual purchases. It spends $40.3 billion through its electronic purchasing systems, and figures its cost avoidance at $405 million, a 10 percent return going right to the bottom line. IBM conducts business with 32,000 suppliers in this manner.

"If a buyer has to touch something manually, there's a defect in the system," according to John Paterson, chief procurement officer for the company.[3]

FedEx is another company heavily in tune with e-commerce. As late as 1998, 5 percent to 10 percent of the people in procurement functions were contributing 70 percent to 80 percent of the strategic value, with the reverse focused only on tactical contributions. Chief sourcing officer Edith Kelly-Green has turned that model upside down, with the focus on strategic initiatives. Of the 170 people in supply chain roles, over half are setting strategic plans for the company. To date, about 25 percent of the FedEx purchase volume has been through their e-commerce process.[4]

This is the advantage of technology, freeing work from the mundane, repetitive tasks and allowing for the creative future planning best done by the human computer. It does not come without a price.

Summary

Plan for the implementation of e-commerce and B2B in your organization. Understand what the potential benefits are, and where the traps might be hidden. When you think you have a plan in place, and are ready to start the process, don't. Take another pass at your plan, focusing on potential risks. Know where you are going, the expected benefits, and the costs to be faced.

E-commerce is not easy at first, and there will be ramifications to your organization you may not have considered. Sourcing staff might be affected, as well as internal logistics. If you feel the need for more convincing, consider this. According to a study by Forrest Research, as reported in *BusinessWeek* magazine, "Forty percent of companies that adopted programs to manage the inevitable change in processes when they installed online systems reduced their costs. In contrast, only 3 percent of companies that didn't do so saved money."[5] If the planning is done as part of a carefully thought-out, front-end process, the total benefit derived to the organization will be significant.

Notes

1. Robert D. Hof and Steve Hamm, "How E-Biz Rose, Fell, and Will Risc Anew," *BusinessWeek* magazine (May 13, 2002), p. 64.
2. www.ariba.com.
3. Douglas A. Smock, "Best Practices at Big Blue Three Years Later," *Purchasing* (February 21, 2002), p. 11.
4. Susan Avery, "E-Procurement Delivers for FedEx," *Purchasing* (October 18, 2001), p. 72.
5. Hof and Hamm, op cit.

How to Compete with the Big Dogs

THERE ARE NO UNIVERSALS, even in the world of sourcing books, and this one is no exception. Many companies face unique situations in their daily business lives, and like a universal, one-size-fits-all glove that really doesn't, the same is true with sourcing. There is no one-size-fits-all strategy. The trick is to determine what will work and to customize it to your own needs.

Just Because You're Not G.M. Doesn't Mean You Can't Compete

This book's focus is directed at businesses with under $100 million in sales, a segment of industry that makes up about 98 percent of nongovernment businesses in the United States.[1]

Regrettably, the business owner or sourcing specialist, looking through the magazines and many books on purchasing, can quickly become discouraged by the focus on the big dogs. In reviewing some of the current articles, one is faced with a barrage of news on what companies the likes of General Motors, Abbott Laboratories, John

Deere, Ford Motor, and Caterpillar are doing. The authors come across as breathless with excitement over the latest Internet auction held by one of these behemoth companies, or how they have worked with a large supplier and achieved direct-to-location shipments to all their sites. I recently read about annual targets in purchase cost savings in the neighborhood of $1 billion or more for a number of large companies. One billion dollars in cost savings is ten times more than the total annual sales of almost every one of the industrial companies in the country. Make no mistake, this is all very exciting news, and it is an indicator of the future possibilities to be attained by a creative sourcing department.

Unfortunately, the harsh reality for the largest number of companies in industrial America, and the audience of this book, is that there is very little interest in an auction site for the average company's needs, no matter what the commodity. Ford Motor Company's annual purchase is $90 billion, the largest spend in corporate America. General Motors is next, with $86 billion, followed by Enron (was $60 billion), and Exxon Mobil Corporation with $52.5 billion.[2] Even a business on the high side of the spectrum addressed here will still have only a few purchases in excess of $1 million annually, a level not likely to attract key suppliers populating the auction sites on the Web.

Opportunities to be derived by today's growth in e-commerce and electronic business still remain elusive for the smaller player. The challenge is for companies to be creative in identifying profitable and efficient niches to exploit.

You will likely not garner a lot of attention to a Web site auction for your cardboard needs, for example. That doesn't preclude you from searching the Web for new, more efficient suppliers with the tools and experience to work with you in a more effective, cost-saving manner. Look for the local supplier with warehouse capabilities to stock your products. Perhaps other companies in the area use similar boxes, and the supplier can double up on his orders, creating mutual efficiencies. Be on the lookout for a growing vendor who can supply a broader spectrum of your needs.

Every company you deal with that allows you to enter orders and check stock and status electronically is a significant potential cost-saving opportunity for your company. Suppliers with the capability of looking directly into your system to see requirements, and who are willing to plan inventory and deliver as needed, will save you a measurable amount of sourcing dollars in the long run.

The point is that you may not play on the exact same electronic gridiron as the big dogs, but a lot of the technology is easily adapted and available to smaller companies, and you don't have to be a General Motors to use these tools.

Free Consultants

Your suppliers, correctly chosen and committed partners to your success, are an unrecognized and underutilized asset many companies overlook in their daily work.

If you are using a printing house, for example, to run your catalogs and advertising products, chances are that it knows more about putting ink on media than your company will ever know, or care to know. Once you recognize that fact, and accept that this is a resource and not a weakness, you now have a "free" consultant to work with you on current and future projects. All you need do to utilize this valuable asset is determine your objectives and goals, explain your needs, ask your partners for their help, and then let your consultants loose.

In one case, I led involving printing, the customer had about twelve different sizes of card stock it used for its products. When an open-ended question asked how the total card stock costs could be reduced, a simple project was begun to learn all we could about using these stocks. The first point that quickly became apparent was that there were about four core family sizes. Within these family sizes existed similar cards, all within about a quarter-inch of each other in size. The printer's initial recommendation was to group card products within the four families and standardize on one size, thus coming up with a cost savings potential of almost 25 percent.

This number was of such interest to the company that the logical next question asked of this supplier was whether he was aware of any other opportunities.

In all, several areas were identified as potential cost savers, including reviewing the level of print required on the reverse side of the card. Did we really need clear, almost photographic printing, or would sketches and drawing suffice? If so, there were significant cost savings to be had there.

Were we willing to commit to a minimum level of raw material inventory located at the customer's facility? Although, on first blush, this appears to be in conflict with everything we've learned about minimum inventory levels and no contracts, in this case, the investment was six weeks' worth of material. This was material that, in its raw state, could be used in many of our other applications, thus minimizing inventory risks while increasing schedule flexibility. In return, the customer then could negotiate for regular runs of better-quality stock made by his supplier. Quality would improve, and costs would be reduced, all for a very minimal investment in highly usable inventory.

These and other exciting opportunities occurred just because we took the time to ask our expert.

Opportunities in Quality

Often the mere mention of quality has a negative connotation to it, like a bitter policeman looking over your shoulder, ready to pounce on the first mistake you make.

But look carefully at your quality. This is a melting pot of opportunity. Ask yourself a few questions.

❑ Do you have quality specifications? How do you know what you are buying and what your supplier is delivering?

❑ Are you asking for average quality, expecting the best possible, and selling your customer something that might not exist?

❑ Are you properly managing your customers' quality expectations?

Buy the quality level needed, not what is possible. Understand where your product is used and in what manner. A hospital application is, by necessity, one that is considerably higher than that in an auto garage, but is that enough or the only information to have? Even in a hospital environment, a window-washing product used in a non-sterile location, such as the front door and lobby, certainly may not need to meet the same specifications as the product used in the operating room. The goal is to work with suppliers to deliver your true quality needs, not what is theoretically possible.

Vendor–Managed Inventory

One often-overlooked technique for attaining additional advantages in business is vendor scheduling. The actual range of implementation varies from a blanket order for annual goods, to be scheduled, delivered, maintained, and invoiced by your supplier, to providing detailed forecasts and orders, allowing the vendor to determine lot sizes and delivery frequencies, thus optimizing his production runs.

Making this decision requires careful study and analysis from your company and determining a means of benchmarking performance and savings. It also requires developing a cadre of trustworthy partner-vendors to begin the program.

Complete vendor-managed inventory would entail creating a list of items to be supplied by the chosen vendor. Once a mutual understanding of how the process is to work has been reached, and both parties agree to the required commitments, then the process of implementation begins.

The vendor is shown the location each item is to be stocked in, and directed on how to manage that location. Ideally, your company would have determined the proper stocking level to keep in place, and allocated space accordingly. This is the ultimate Kan Ban system. The vendor is directed to fill the square as it best determines, but must make sure the square is never allowed to go below a certain level of inventory, and be certain no material is delivered that would require more space than what is available in the location.

Depending upon the number of items and rates of consumption, the vendor must survey its squares on a frequency so that the inventory goals are met. In some cases, this might mean daily visits.

One last item is that, no matter the frequency of delivery, the vendor is to invoice on a monthly basis only. This will ensure that the savings in material handling and ordering are not offset and consumed by maintaining excess paperwork in accounting.

Opportunities Exist Everywhere

An often-overlooked opportunity to reduce costs and take advantage of volume buying is available through purchasing groups. A quick surf of the Web will lead you to several sites where a group of like companies or organizations have banded together to buy common items in bulk, and at much lower rates. You will discover groups from common industries, educational institutions, unions, and professional and business associations.

In reviewing these groups, I am reminded of credit unions that band together the resources of a group of like-minded individuals, for volume business and to compete effectively with much larger banks. As a member of such a buying group, you might be able to achieve results comparable to your larger competitors.

Fellow purchasing personnel at companies in your own neighborhood are another resource to explore. Buyers face the same common problems, regardless of the particular industry they are in. Sourcing specialists deal with competitive pressures, price squeezes, product availability, and finding new sources, issues common to any industry.

Many of your fellow sourcing professionals may also have come up with creative solutions to the problems they face. These may be easily adaptable to your particular situation. You may have a technique that you use daily, one you might take for granted, that would be very helpful to another buyer in another venue.

The difficulty is one of communication and sharing of information. Why not call your counterparts at another company, suggest areas of common interest, and perhaps set up a quarterly meeting to discuss problems and solutions? Share your concerns and questions across a conference table, and let them share theirs. You might discover a wealth of information, ideas, and techniques that may be beneficial to all.

Also, do not overlook professional groups and associations, such as APICS or the Institute for Supply Management, formerly the National Association of Purchasing Management.

Summary

Many of the efficiencies attained by the largest companies in the business universe are attained by sheer size. Ironically, so are most of their inefficiencies. Try visualizing these companies as being like the supertankers plying their trades on the oceans of the world. Although a model of efficiency in moving millions of barrels of oil from point A to point B, a change in course must be planned long in advance, and still consumes many miles and lots of time to accomplish. This is not the case with the smaller powerboat, which is able to run circles around the lumbering giant, and nimbly remain clear of the crushing bow.

The General Motorses of the world exert a significant amount of influence in the business environment, not only with customers, but also on their suppliers. They are able to wring unheard-of concessions and performance numbers out of their vendors—something smaller competitors cannot do. But this is a double-edged sword, requiring long lead times and billion-dollar commitments by both parties.

As a sourcing specialist for a much smaller company, you can attain significant costs savings by being creative in approaching suppliers. A clear understanding of your product and supplier needs, and the ability to work with suppliers to attain them, will yield very significant rewards to your company's bottom line and your career credibility.

Anyone can compete with the big dogs. The secret is to use creative investments of time and brainpower to replace billion-dollar commitments. Play to win the game on your own turf, with your own strengths, and under your own rules.

Notes

1. www.Bizstats.com/bizsizes98.htm.
2. "Top 250 Purchasing Departments," *Supply Chain Yearbook*, Reed Business Information (2002), p. 88, www.supplychainlink.com.

CHAPTER 14

The Total Cost of Acquisition

EVERY ACTIVITY IN BUSINESS has a cost associated with it, and the sourcing of material is no exception. Ongoing product purchases have direct and indirect costs of procurement. Modern companies understand these as the cost of doing business. It is only by knowing how to measure, capture, and report all costs associated with procuring an item that the total cost of acquisition can be determined.

There are two kinds of costs that a sourcing specialist should be aware of. The first is purchase price, a component of standard cost, which normally consists of the purchase price and a material overhead percentage added by finance to account for the normal expenses of doing business.

The second is the total cost of acquisition, which takes into account variables that come into play by doing business with one supplier versus another. These costs are estimates created by actual experience or best guess. We are interested in exploring this total cost of acquisition.

Once the components that go into total costs are known and understood, it is easier to track and report the relative performance levels of competing suppliers.

Components of Standard Cost

There are several associated costs with order placement, some obvious, some perhaps not quite so. A purchased part will be carried on the books at most companies at a standard cost. This value consists of the actual purchase price, plus various overheads added as a percentage, to account for other associated costs. A few examples of apparent (and less apparent) contributors to overhead costs are discussed below.

Note that the following items are representative of the indirect costs associated with most departments within a company. These amounts are used to calculate a material overhead rate, which is then added to prime material price as a component of total standard cost. There may be other charges, but these serve as a good example.

Information Systems

Some form of computer and information systems supports the majority of companies. The costs associated with the purchase, maintenance, and depreciation of the hardware is one segment. Another is the cost of the operators, technicians, programmers, and administrators to run the system. There is also the cost of the space occupied, and its share of utilities.

Communications

Telephone equipment, fax machines, pagers, and cell phones, for example, incur similar charges as information systems.

Occupied Space

For companies that allocate space charges, part of the material or sourcing overhead will reflect costs relating to the occupied facilities. The makeup of these charges might include insurance, depreciation, maintenance, equipment, and utilities.

Labor

The labor in placing an order includes not only the allocated portion of departmental labor, but also the benefits of the buyer, plus the costs of related support personnel, such as filing clerks or expediters.

Supplies

When placing purchase orders, there are expenses such as preprinted purchase order forms, desktop computer paper, and equipment maintenance. The costs involved also include physically handling the purchase order forms, making required revisions, and mailing charges.

Total Cost of Acquisition

It is imperative that sourcing specialists understand the difference between purchase price and total cost of acquisition. Making purchase decisions based solely on purchase price is shortsighted and inefficient, and could be indicative of an inexperienced, poorly trained, or unprofessional sourcing function.

Several factors make up the total cost of acquisition, and all of them need to be carefully looked at and understood before a final recommendation is made, particularly in the case of a new item, or a new vendor.

Figure 1 is a chart that can be easily used as a planning and decision-making tool for determining total cost of acquisition. It takes into account most of the critical and relevant factors of total costs. It also is in a format readily adaptable to a spreadsheet program where the numbers can be plugged in and a total quickly arrived at. You might find other areas to be added, or segments that may not apply to your situation. Change it as your requirements dictate.

Figure 2 is a table loaded with sample data showing how the total cost of acquisition process may be used to compare multiple suppliers, and it demonstrates three different quoted purchase prices for the same item. The numbers include accounting for expected or historical reject rate. Costs are also included for in-house reworking of the material, transportation and freight charges, cost of late deliveries to your plant, special handling fees, and credit for vendor-managed inventory.

By quickly looking at the resulting numbers, it is clear that Company "C," although the lowest-purchase-priced supplier in this example, is actually the most expensive vendor to do business with on a total-cost basis. Although its purchase price is at least 5 percent less than the next highest competitor, on a total-cost basis it exceeds Company "B" by more than thirty-two cents, or 26 percent.

The important point is that Company "B" is the proper choice to

FIGURE 1

Vendor Name: _____

Item Number: _____ Desc: _____

	Data	Total
Purchase Price		_____
Typical Lot Size	_____	
Transportation		
2% Ship Point	_____	_____
0% Destination	_____	_____
Vendor-Managed Inventory		
−2.5%	_____	_____
Late Delivery		
Days Late X	_____	
(25% X Day)	_____	_____
Rework Charge		
Percentage of Lot X Price	_____	_____
Reject Charge		
Percentage of Lot X Price	_____	_____
Administration Fee		
$25 per Lot	_____	_____
Material Handling		
$55 per Hour	_____	_____
Miscellaneous	_____	_____
Total Cost of Acquisition		$_____

FIGURE 2

Vendor Name:	Company A		Company B		Company C	
	Data	Total	Data	Total	Data	Total
Purchase Price		$1.00		$1.20		$0.95
Typical Lot Size	1000		1000		1000	
Reject Cost						
Percentage of Lot	9%	$.09	2%	$.02	15%	$.14
Rework Charge						
Percentage of Lot	100%	$.09	100%	$.02	100%	$.14
Transportation						
2% FOB Ship Point 0%	0%		2%	$.02	0%	
0% FOB Destination						
Late Delivery						
Average Days Late	.5	$.125	0	$.0	1	$.24
25% Per Day						
Extra Miscellaneous Fees	0	$.0	0	$.0	$25	$.03
Vendor-Managed Inventory	Yes	$.025 −	No	$.0	Yes	$.024 −
− 2.5% / Month						
Total Cost of Acquisition		$1.280		$1.260		$1.476

do business with. Although its purchase price is not the lowest, the total cost of acquisition is. On a day-in, day-out basis, "B" will be the lowest-cost provider to your company.

These are by no means the only charges that might be considered in doing a total cost of acquisition analysis. If, for example, your supplier's plant is at a distant location from your facility, prudence may direct that you purchase and maintain a level of safety stock inventory to cover short-term fluctuations in demand, or the uncertainty of en route transportation schedules. There is a cost associated with this decision, and it can be added into the equation.

Another consideration might be packaging material for the product. A local supplier may well be able to recycle and reuse its own delivery medium, whereas a remote supplier may require sturdier materials to withstand the rigors of long-distance shipping. This could create additional handling and disposal issues for your company, a definite expense to be added to the total cost.

The chart is an effective tool for taking into account as many variations of the cost of procurement analysis as possible, utilizing an objective, quantitative methodology. Properly used, it is an excellent means for determining the lowest-cost supplier.

Cost of Rejected Material

By using this same analysis format, it is easy to determine the cost of rejected material, and use the calculation as a basis for debiting your supplier on a cost of quality basis.

Assume for the moment that an entire lot of material from Company "A" has been rejected, and the disposition is to return it to the vendor. Not taking into account the impact to the production line, and assuming that replacement material was readily at hand, the chart data could be revised as shown in Figure 3.

In this example, we are using the same data and format. There are some different assumptions made here. The reject and rework costs must be zero dollars. Although the entire lot is being rejected, full credit for the purchase price will be expected. In addition, since the lot has been characterized as return to vendor (RTV), there are no rework charges incurred.

However, there are additional charges associated with returning product. One is a documentation fee to create the debit memo, obtain a return material authorization from the vendor, and process the required inventory adjustments. In this example, there is a flat documentation fee of twenty-five dollars.

Rejected material was also removed from either the production line or incoming inspection areas when it was determined as not meeting standards. It had to be identified and segregated, moved to a proper holding area, and stored. There are material handling charges involved in this process, which the example assumes to be fifty-five dollars per hour, the factory-burdened labor rate. In this example, although the direct purchase price was one dollar each, the additional charges for handling and documentation increase the cost of the rejected material to $1.165 each. This is the total cost to your company for having ordered this item. Under differing conditions, there may be other charges to apply, changing the outcome.

Although this process might have to be negotiated and agreed upon up front, these are valid charges to apply to a vendor who has

FIGURE 3

Vendor Name:	Company A Data	Total
Purchase Price		$ 1.00
Reject Cost Percentage of Lot	8%	$ 0.00
Rework Charge Percentage of Lot	100%	$ 0.00
Transportation 2% FOB Ship Point	0%	$ 0.00
Late Delivery Average Days Late 25% Per Day	.0	$ 0.00
Extra Miscellaneous Fees	$ 25	$ .03
Vendor-Managed Inventory − 2.5%/Month	N/A	$ .00
Document Processing $25 Document Prep 2-Hour Material Handling @ $55/Hour	$ 25 $110	$ .025 $ .11
Total Reject Cost		$ 1.165
(Debit Memo Amount)		$1,165.00

not performed to specification. More importantly to you, they represent a true cost of purchasing the product from this supplier.

Summary

The total cost of purchased materials is never the purchase price alone, and the lowest-cost vendor may not be the vendor offering the lowest purchase price. What is presented in this chapter is a clear tool to make logical, quantitative decisions, taking into account as many factors affecting cost as possible.

Using the same process, the means of determining a total cost of quality, relative to a given supplier's product or delivery, can also be derived. For too long, the total costs of the equation have been overlooked, in favor of purchase price alone. A stricter, more detailed cost analysis tool must be at hand to undertake a complete analysis of the data, thus increasing the probability of arriving at the correct recommendation. The formulas and processes presented in this chapter will help out immensely.

CHAPTER 15

Lead Time

ASK A HALF DOZEN PEOPLE in sourcing to define "lead time," and I would wager that you will get seven definitions. This ambiguity is not their fault.

Between software engineers trying to come up with innovative systematic solutions, marketing and sales people creating problems for which they hope to sell the solution, and users convinced that the problems they face every day are unique and have no solution, we have managed to completely cloud the topic and issues related to lead time.

Components of Lead Time

Taking a simplistic approach for the moment, let us define lead time as the amount of time it takes from when a demand for a specific component is created until such time as it is delivered to its required stockroom or appropriate location, and made available for consumption.

From a sourcing perspective, and for purposes of illustration, lead time begins when the requirement shows up on your desk. Your first step is to obtain any required approvals before placing the order. The vendor will then schedule and ship the product to you, where it is delivered to your receiving dock. The next step would include required inspection before putting the data into your company's system, followed by delivery to its stockroom or floor location. The time it took to complete this process, from beginning to end, is total lead time.

Some of the more interesting components of lead time, all in the example above, represent areas that a sourcing specialist should be concerned with. In addition, the sourcing specialist should clearly understand their unique ramifications.

If your process requires certain dollar-limit, management-level approvals prior to order placement, it impacts lead time, and you need to account for this. How long does it take to get the requisition to the correct person? How long does the requisition sit on a desk until it is approved, and then returned to you? In some organizations, this process can take a week or more. This is an inefficient process, but it is a component of total lead time. If your company does not allow placing of the order pending proper sign-off, which from a legal standpoint it would probably insist on, then the delivery clock from the vendor can't start ticking until the completed paperwork is returned.

Getting the order to the supplier is another area to consider. Many suppliers quote lead time as after receipt of order, or ARO. This means its lead-time clock doesn't start ticking until it has the specifics of the purchase order in hand. For some companies, a phone call is adequate; for others, it is not. Can you fax the order, or send it electronically? That certainly saves time, and doesn't add to the process. But if a hard copy of an original document is necessary, then lead time must account for paperwork in-transit time.

Other components of manufacturing lead time include queue, or wait time. The time the purchase order sits on a manager's desk awaiting approval is queue time. So is the time a part is stored in front of the next operation in a manufacturing shop. Over the years, many studies have documented that upwards of 90 percent or more of manufacturing lead time is actually queue time, with no actual work performed on the part. If lead time were ten days, nine of those days were spent in a wait state.

Lead time also includes the time that product sits on shipping and receiving docks, the time spent waiting for trucks to pick up the product, travel time, and the time expended waiting to be received on a system. It also includes the time to be delivered and put away to a stockroom (including a Kan Ban location on the floor).

The lead-time pie can be muddied further by negative queue time and lot control. Negative queue time is loaded into a multilevel manufacturing bill of materials when a lower-level part is used on a higher-level assembly. In this case, the queue time of the higher part is in the total wait time, so the queue time of the lower-level part is shown as a negative number, since it is assumed there is only one queue time in the process.

Lot size control is utilized where any specific part needs to be tracked through the whole manufacturing or ordering process for accountability purposes. In this case, a handful of parts may be completed at one station in the process. Now the parts are ready to be shipped. However, everything must wait for the completion of the very last part in the lot. This is done so that the entire batch can be moved as one and, thus, is easier to trace.

How Fixed Is Fixed Lead Time?

The reality is that lead time is whatever you say it is. After the example above, you are justified in being skeptical, but in certain instances, it is true.

Back in the halcyon days of high tech in Silicon Valley, it felt as if every company in electronic land was earning an obscene amount of money. As a result, it was a commonly held belief that any manufacturing or engineering problem would go away if only enough dollars were thrown at it.

This mentality especially applied to manufacturing lead times from critical suppliers. When the customer was willing to pay for it, most suppliers were willing to deliver product in short order and outside normal production cycles. Ten weeks of lead time could disappear if the sourcing manager was willing to spend the money required to make it so. The fact was that critical material shortage lead times were affected by whoever had the most expediting dollars dripping out of his pocket.

Poor planning at the front end of the process drove most of these situations. Customer commitments were made in the blind, with no availability information at hand. Competitive pressures dictated that if one company could not supply the end product, there were others out there willing to take on the task. Another heavy influence was the out-of-control competitive egos unwilling to lose a sale, no matter the cost or disruption to normal distribution channels.

Overnight Delivery to the Rescue

A willing contributor to this bad planning cycle (and one reason it took so long to be addressed) was the emergence of the overnight delivery services. Companies such as FedEx offered bandages in the form of vans and jets. They owed their very existence to the dual-headed god of bad planning and lead-time reduction. An extremely effective, dollar-driven, incredibly expensive solution, these companies played into the emotional hand-wringing surrounding the industry. The unspoken message was that the smiling delivery driver in a red-and-blue truck would ride to your rescue and save you from the failure of poor planning. Federal Express and other overnight delivery providers became huge corporations by providing crutches on wings.

Even today, when most of the flexibility has been squeezed out of the length of time it takes to receive product, and customer priorities are actual (instead of set by price point, competition, or ego), lead time can still be manipulated.

An effective, cost-driven process demands setting real priorities for all orders. At the same time, a team of technical, marketing, and manufacturing personnel should investigate how they can change the demand, or the product, to shorten the lead times and improve customer availability.

A constant goal of a good sourcing person is to look for opportunities to reduce lead times wherever possible. The first place to start is with the team approach, reviewing each product.

Why Lead-Time Reductions?

What are some of the reasons you would want reduced lead times?

❑ **Reduced Costs.** If, like most companies, you receive parts FOB factory, you have the title and liability for the goods at the time they are loaded on the truck. This could be a week or more before you actually receive the parts.

❑ **Changes in Demand.** The longer a part is in process, the greater the risk of changes in demand. The order driving the demand could be canceled, rescheduled, or changed before the components even reach your facility.
❑ **The Risk of Obsolescence.** The longer it takes to be available, the greater the risk of an in-process design change. If you have to hold significant levels of safety stock to cover fluctuating demand, the risk is increased further.
❑ **Improved Customer Service.** The closer your supply point is to your customer demand, the more likely the product will actually be sold to the customer, reducing order cancellations.

The Lead-Time Reduction Process

Like many other tasks in this book, reducing lead time is an evolutionary process requiring several steps. Many are quite similar to other process reviews, such as cost reduction and vendor consolidation. Some of the key steps include:

❑ **Reviewing Product Specifications.** Are they too tight for the actual usage of the component? Are you buying a premium part, when a standard would meet the needs of the customer or end product?
❑ **Complexity.** Are there opportunities to reduce the complexity of the part, thereby reducing the amount of labor and manufacturing process time required to make the item?
❑ **Part Commonality.** Is there a more common part that might be designed in, increasing availability and reducing cost and lead-time?
❑ **Consolidation of Design.** Can two or more parts be combined into a single, lower-cost, more efficient part?
❑ **Material.** Can a lower-cost, more readily available material be used in the making of the part in question?
❑ **Proximity.** The closer a source is to the consuming point, the better the chance of reducing lead time. Shortened transportation times always figure into the equation. The same city is

better than the same state, the state better than the country, the country better than the rest of the world.

Study the use, function, materials, specifications, and quality requirements for possible simplification and resulting lead-time reduction.

Summary

Lead-time management is becoming a significant contributor to success within the sourcing world. Reducing lead time is an important component of improved customer service and reduced inventory investment. It will become a critical measurement of the effectiveness of sourcing departments as time moves forward. A thorough knowledge of lead time, its components, and possible available steps to reduce it will help assure your sourcing success in the future.

CHAPTER 16

Buy Capacity, Not Parts

IF CALLED UPON to identify the one, most successful sourcing skill, I would not hesitate to respond that it is the ability and willingness to think creatively when faced with a problem or opportunity. A buyer possessing this skill would never settle for the trite, obvious, or pat solution to a problem. She would, instead, exhibit a willingness to work with her suppliers to stimulate problem-solving skills and come up with a new, creative solution to the issue before them.

One such technique of which I am particularly fond, and one practiced with far less frequency in sourcing than it should be, is to think of yourself as buying capacity, not parts.

Lead Time and Capacity

The seed of this idea was planted in my mind at a seminar I attended in the early 1990s in Portland, Oregon. Roger Brooks, a principal of Ollie Wight LLC, was leading a discussion of the components of lead time in a factory environment.[1]

As he explained, if we consider factory throughput to be analogous to a large funnel, then all of the components of factory lead time will be represented. (See Figure 4.)

FIGURE 4

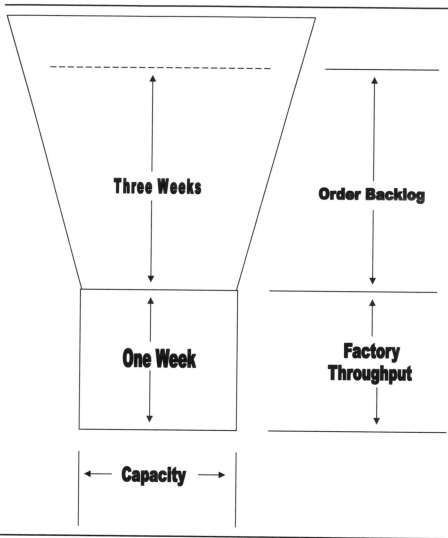

Three Weeks

Order Backlog

One Week

Factory
Throughput

Capacity

Throughput is factory capacity, and is represented by the diameter of the narrowest part of the narrow end of the funnel. No matter how hard you push, you cannot get more material through this part than physically allowed by the size of the opening. A fire hose pressed into a half-inch funnel will still yield only a half-inch stream of water.

The length of the narrow part of the funnel is the sum total of actual work time in the factory. This is the time the part is being moved, staged, or actually on a machine having work done to it.

The ever-narrowing bowl leading to the spout represents the backlog of orders. When customer orders are poured into this end at a faster rate than orders are completed out the other end of the spout, the backlog will grow. Throughput is not increased, and the speed of the actual machine process is not affected, by the amount of water poured into the bowl. Simply put, the more the bowl fills up, the longer it takes an order to get through the entire process, and the greater total lead time becomes. The narrow end of the funnel remains the limiting choke point affecting throughput.

The only way for a factory to affect lead time is to change the size of the output spout. Shortening the required process length, improving factory efficiency, or making a larger funnel, adding more capacity, are the only two ways to accomplish this goal.

Start with the Wrong Assumptions

Buying capacity can be a difficult concept to grasp at first. Once the light goes on, it becomes instinctively logical but remains difficult to explain and implement. In spite of this, it is a very rewarding process when done correctly.

The easiest way to demonstrate buying capacity is to draw our huge funnel on a flip chart–size page. (See Figure 5.) If we fill it two-thirds full on the reservoir end, and draw a line there, we will assume that from this spot to the output of the spout on the bottom of the page will represent four weeks of lead time. Let's further assume there are three weeks in the deep end, waiting for work, and about seven days in the narrow end, being processed.

Keeping our funnel in mind, let's walk through a typical capacity process that can get buyers and suppliers into difficulty, if they are not careful. Then we will see how buying capacity might alleviate the problem.

FIGURE 5

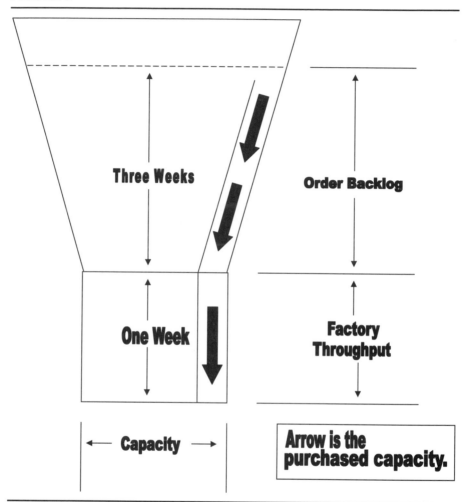

Assume your critical supplier owns the funnel we've just drawn, and it is representative of its factory process. Your company consumes about 10 percent of its total business, both in dollars and capacity. You are faced with placing orders at least four weeks before you expect delivery, but notice the bowl is filling up a bit, so you have started placing orders five weeks out, just in case.

We just created problem number one. With no change in total

demand, the buyer has poured more water into the bowl, increasing the apparent backlog at his supplier's level.

Take a Leap of Faith

Your supplier begins to see five weeks of backlog in the bowl of its funnel, and starts quoting five weeks delivery to all of its customers. Being smart and alert buyers, they place more orders, filling the bowl even more.

Nothing has really changed in the equation. Factory capacity remains the same as it has always been. Throughput has not changed. Price and quality remain constant, and the actual order rate has not increased. But perceived lead time has gone from four to five weeks. Being a very aware sourcing specialist, you spot this trend, and just to be safe and show your boss how on top of the situation you are, you start placing your orders out for six weeks. And the chain continues to lengthen. Nothing has changed, but quoted delivery lead times have increased 50 percent.

We are now faced with problem number two. The increased backlog is sending false signals to the supplier and the customer base.

Jump to the Wrong Conclusions

Your supplier notes the increase in backlog and assumes business is growing. Because of your long-term relationship, your vendor offers to keep your orders at four weeks, but for a modest increase in price. Now, something has changed in the equation. You are paying more for your components.

We have now experienced problem number three, an increase in price.

At the same time your vendor is making this generous offer to you, it looks at the bowl at the top of the funnel, notes that the backlog level has increased from four weeks to six, and quickly concludes that there is an increase in sustained business. Lengthening lead times may force customers to begin looking to other products and solutions. This is a concern to the supplier, since it really wants to keep all the business it worked so hard to acquire in the first place. Rather than risk losing business, the vendor decides to increase capacity by hiring more people, adding more shifts, and maybe beginning to plan for new facilities.

We've arrived at problem number four. Incomplete data and misunderstood signals are driving premature and erroneous capacity decisions.

A good illustration of the phenomena I am presenting is the electronic semiconductor industry, historically notorious for creating phantom demand and backlog. The usual scenario features companies beginning to see the book-to-bill ratio, an industrywide standard report comparing orders placed to orders shipped, slowly edging upward. A ratio of one indicates new orders are replacing orders shipped one-for-one. A higher ratio indicates that demand and backlog are growing, perhaps greater than capacity, and if the trend continues, at some point, lead times will likely increase. A rapidly increasing book-to-bill ratio sends fear into the hearts of electronic buyers, who, in order to protect their hide, begin placing the same demand with multiple suppliers, increasing backlog and lead times, and contributing further to a growing, yet phantom, demand.

Once the first delivery is made by whichever supplier is able to perform, all other duplicate orders will be quickly cancelled. In the time it takes to place a few phone calls killing these orders, huge backlogs disappear, and lead times are reduced from months to weeks almost overnight.

Buying Capacity

Let's try buying capacity instead of parts, and look again at Figure 5.

Along the inside edge of your funnel, draw a distinct line that parallels the shape of the funnel, and represents about 10 percent of the area of the narrow end. This area between the funnel edge and the line you've just drawn represents the amount of your supplier's business that you purchase week in and week out. This is the capacity that you are buying and your vendor is dedicating to your products.

Demonstrate this scenario to your supplier, suggesting that you would like to place orders buying this same capacity every week. You want to determine the exact makeup, whether part numbers or configurations, that requires this capacity at the last possible moment in its manufacturing process. Working together, you should discover when this point actually occurs. This becomes your new order placement time.

A decorative foam-stamping pad was a product we procured from an overseas source at one company I worked for. It consisted of a design face, approximately one-eighth-inch thick, which might consist of a multitude of colors. A Christmas tree, for example, would require green foam for the body, red globes, and a white ball at the top. The design was then glued to a black foam backing, approximately one-half-inch thick. The overall design size might be up to five inches or more square. It was used to transfer paint to a flat surface. There were approximately 800 designs actively sold, with an annual volume in excess of 6 million units.

Normal procedures had my company place orders for the product in 2,500-lot size minimums, four weeks before they were scheduled to be shipped. They were then loaded into containers for the three-week trip across the Pacific, spending another week to clear customs and be delivered to our factory, where we broke down the delivery, either shipping product out to customers or putting it away in our stockroom.

Total lead time to a customer delivery for product we did not have on hand could extend up to ten or twelve weeks, much too long for our customers who expected delivery within a few weeks of their order placement with us.

We decided to attack this as a capacity problem and see where we might be able to make improvements. The first thing we knew was that our average weekly buy, ignoring seasonality of demand for the moment, was 120,000 units. At the supplier level, we knew that 80 percent of the raw material demand was in the black foam backing, less than 20 percent in the colored foam used in the design. A further breakdown indicated that about 80 percent of the colored foam was in basic colors, such as red, green, yellow, and white.

With the availability of this data, how could we both work toward reducing manufacturing lead time? The answer was to buy capacity, not foam stamps.

After working with the supplier, we committed to purchase a fixed minimum of stamps every week. Its total capacity was over a million stamps, so we were not taking up an undue amount of the supplier's sales capacity that might affect its other customers. The vertically integrated vendor would maintain production to ensure that there was plenty of black foam backing material available, along with minimum amounts required of colored stock. With this commitment from us, the question to be answered was at what point did the vendor require us to define the final designs?

Careful study revealed that it took only three days to stamp out the designs, glue them to the backing, and package them for shipment. The rest of the process time was taken up in either manufacturing raw foam or in queue time, when material awaited the next operation. It was apparent that we could determine the final design requirements and quantities one week prior to shipment.

By working with the vendor and buying capacity, not foam stamps, we were able to reduce the required manufacturing portion of the total lead time by three weeks, or 75 percent.

Benefits of Buying Capacity

The benefits of this effort were many, and included reduced levels of safety stock on site in case (Just-in-Case inventory) the actual demand differed from the long-range forecast. Utilization of inventory investment improved significantly, because product was made closer to the final customer demand point. And since the two decision points were closer together, the supplier received far fewer calls requesting changes to its production schedule when actual customer orders differed from forecast.

There are other ways to successfully utilize this concept. If you know your company's products and demands the way a successful sourcing specialist must, then you will understand the components that are required to build them. Do a study of and find the highest level of commonality involved. In other words, what component is common to all the variables that might exist in your finished goods? You might discover a multitude of parts and items used across a number of product families in your company.

One company I know used tens of millions of labels on their products. Some were used only a few thousand per year; other labels hundreds of thousands per week. Label material also varied to about ten different configurations.

In studying this case, your first instinct based on past purchasing practices might be to stratify the labels by quantity used per year, and negotiate a deal with your supplier to gain a better price due to volume, or to run specific quantities each time to ensure that your company will never run out of material.

This is certainly a logical approach, and one that historically has been very successful. However, in pursuing the creative solution track and taking the thought process to its next level, other avenues came to mind. One possibility was to approach the label supplier, not in the usual manner of number of labels per design and quantity, but total number of labels by size and material. This certainly would be more indicative of total business dollars spent with that vendor. But, taking it one step further, what if the professional sourcing specialist approached the supplier with the total number of square inches in the procurement plan, with final size and design to be provided later? This creative, yet logical progression might provide the basis for some very interesting and fruitful conversations between both parties.

Of course, these are not the only possible approaches to take, and not necessarily the best ones. Instead, they suggest a few of the possibilities inherent in the buy capacity concept.

Summary

Creative, successful lead-time management is a winning strategy for all parties involved, and will become an even more critical component of sourcing success measurements in the future. Buying capacity, instead of parts, will be a major contributor in the march to achieve these goals.

Note

1. Roger Brooks, Oliver Wight, LLC, Oliver Wight Americas, Info @ollie.com.

CHAPTER 17

Contracts: Efficient Freeway or Muddy Morass?

I AM NOT AN AUTHORITY on the legal details and all the ins and outs of creating and managing contracts. I do not present myself as an expert, or even a well-trained user of contracts and purchasing agreements. If this is an area you are particularly interested in, there are many school courses, seminars, and a number of detailed desk references on contracts and purchasing law.

My goal is to discuss the philosophy behind contracts and doing business under the umbrella of purchasing agreements. I will cover common thinking behind the desire to have agreements in place, expectations for process and results, and finally, some thoughts and recommendations regarding contracts.

The assumed goal of a well-written contract is to clearly delineate the expectations, roles, and terms of how two or more companies will do business together. Such contracts are particularly useful when:

❑ The terms and conditions are complex.
❑ Payment vehicles are outside of the normal process.
❑ Long distances separate buyer and seller.
❑ Difficult time lines and project milestones are in place.

❑ There are issues of technological uniqueness, or other protections required of property, characteristics, or design.

❑ Patent or copyright issues may be involved.

Under these conditions, very clear performance expectations of both parties should be documented in a well-written contract.

Do You Need a Contract?

If circumstances include some of the issues noted above, a contract might make perfect sense and be the most efficient umbrella under which to conduct your business.

In general, however, too many contracts are written when a clearly understood business plan would suffice. The following conditions, for example, may not warrant a contract:

❑ When the products involved are standard commodities.

❑ The terms and conditions follow generally accepted practices.

❑ Two or more companies are committed to becoming, or continuing, as long-term partners.

Under these circumstances, the time and effort required of putting every little business nuance down on paper would best be expended in improving the business relationship.

It is vitally important that every sourcing specialist know the total cost of acquisition of his products. This is a keystone to the performance of a professional. A seasoned buyer will thus be confident that he has done all he could to understand the costs of buying from a given supplier. Further, the buyer will know that the pricing and service obtained is the best possible for his company, that the terms are competitive, and that the seeds have been planted for a long-term, growing partnership.

To get to this point, the buying professional will have estimated not only the purchase price, but also the other costs associated with acquisition, including freight, handling, estimated reject and inspection costs, lot size, and costs to carry inventory. He will have priced out any differences between the quantities required and the vendor's minimum lot sizes, and he will have looked at expected lead time, payment terms, and ease of placing orders. The total cost of acquisition form (Figure 1 in Chapter 14) is a great checklist to ensure everything possible has been checked and verified.

In any agreement, it is also imperative to address the needs of your supplier. As part of the process, you will have already assured your supplier that it is entering a true partnership with your company. As a valued partner, you will make every effort to share critical information with it at regular meetings, alternating sites in order to facilitate improved communications. Finally, you must assure your vendor that, although you will occasionally get calls from competitors offering a slight price reduction on a given item, you will ignore those calls, acknowledging you are already obtaining the best combination price and performance package available. If each of these steps were carefully addressed, then the execution of a contract would prove of minimal value.

The Downside of Contracts

If you can agree that the only constant in business is change, then a written contract offers the potential to stand in the way of progress. If not carefully monitored, a contract has a tendency to take on a life of its own. Instead of assuring business stability, contracts can become impediments to future success. As unforeseen opportunities arise, a contract might end up a blockade to progress, instead of a tool directed toward achieving continued mutual success.

In difficult times, it becomes too easy for one party to hunker down behind obscure terms and conditions, utilizing the dark corners of weasel words, instead of sitting down in a trusting atmosphere and genuinely trying to work out a new, potentially successful business direction.

A new process or product may also be placed at risk by this negative approach. When a creative idea arises, the opportunity for both parties to benefit might be overlooked due to a shortsighted commitment to a current product or process, as spelled out in a contract. Instead of both parties deciding to take the risks and do the work to attain a longer-range goal, one or both become adamant about maintaining the current technology. The same is true of investments in inventory and processes that might have to change to meet future demands.

Labor union contracts are often cited as examples of standing in the way of change and progress. The intent of a labor contract is often valid. It is a tool to systemize, standardize, and maintain work and jobs for employees. It is an attempt to ensure that employees are treated honestly and on the same plane.

Where this intent has lost focus and become a blocking force occurs when the contract and job protection stand in the way of progress and change, particularly when faced with competitive pressures. One example that comes to mind was the insistence of the railroad unions on keeping a fireman in the cab of a diesel locomotive. The fireman was the person who shoveled the coal or loaded the wood into the firebox of a steam locomotive. It was a function eliminated with the advent of the diesel-electric locomotive. For years after the technological switch, a fireman rode in the cab of every train, exercising no duties, yet receiving full pay.

The end result was that the labor contract that preserved the job of fireman stood in the way of progress, contributing a nonvalue-added expense to the operating costs and adversely affecting the competitive position of the railroads.

Experience dictates that it is usually easier to talk about new directions candidly across a clear table, without a pile of paper blocking the view. Frank discussions of risk, investment, and future opportunities are the best means to attain future growth and profitability.

If You Must Have a Contract

If the situation dictates that you should negotiate a contract, the final step is to ensure that all due diligence has been applied to the contract proposal, regardless of who initiated the actual document. Key management personnel must review the agreements, including perhaps the CFO, COO, and even CEO, as appropriate. Corporate legal representatives should have a look at it for unforeseen loopholes or risks. There is always the chance that some obscure clause or footnote could rise to become a major business impediment in the future.

As the buyer, you do not want to put yourself in the position as final judge as to the fitness of the contract, or take on the responsibility of making the legal commitment for your company. Under the Universal Commercial Code (U.C.C.) and other common law, there are protections against unforeseen errors and omissions, but legal redress is time-consuming, expensive, and nonvalue-added activity for any company. Feel free to make recommendations and suggestions, but leave the final signatures to those in a better position to understand the implications of company commitments.

Before this occurs, you have the responsibility to carefully review the proposal, ensure its applicability, and make a final recommendation. You will have taken the steps noted above regarding the specifics of quantities, terms, lead times, freight, and product specifications. You should also double-check all the information with the users. Talk with engineering to verify that it is not a product scheduled to be replaced in the near term. Check with marketing for continued sales forecasts, noting growing or declining trends.

Next, check that what is written clearly reflects your understanding of what the two companies have already agreed to. Does it reflect the terms of payment, shipping schedule, quantity and quality specifications, packaging, and other items you have already worked out in preceding negotiations? Verbal understandings in conflict with written terms carry little weight. Ask questions of the agreement when such a perceived difference might exist, and work it out in the final draft.

A successful negotiation session should result in no surprises when the final contract proposal is put on the table. What is in writing should reflect what has been worked out and agreed to verbally by both parties.

Along the same lines, those paragraphs of legal jargon, boilerplate to many, carry the same weight in terms of applicability and enforceability as the rest of the agreement, and must be understood by all parties involved. Read it carefully and make every effort to understand it. The devil is in the details.

The Ten-Minute-More Analysis

After all is said and done, and you feel confident that you have the right plan in place, and that your proposal is the best possible for all concerned, undertake the ten-minute-more analysis.

Mentally take a step back from the whole process, divorce yourself from all the work and effort that has gone into making the document, bury your assumptions, and review it step by step one last time. In coming up with a plan or agreement, it is easy to get so lost in the details and negotiations that some critical step is overlooked, or an erroneous assumption is made. By taking one last pass through the process, step by step and from beginning to end, you quite likely will discover some point or assumption that has been overlooked, or that might not work under the final terms and conditions.

One technique that is particularly effective is to review the contract process in reverse order. Begin your review at the end of the proposed contract process, and work backward to the beginning of the process. Think in terms of where you are, and what it took to get to that specific step in the process. Then take it backward one step, review that position, and take it backward another step, and so on. Do this until you arrive at the beginning of the process. This will make you think carefully of exactly how each step leads to the next step, promoting a clearer understanding of the flow of the proposed agreement.

The time to identify errors of misunderstanding or omission is before the agreement is signed. It is much easier to correct oversights before, rather than after, the agreement has been put in force. Not only will everyone find it easier to save face, but also the integrity of the process becomes stronger when all the identified weaknesses can be addressed, and all issues worked out ahead of signing.

Nondisclosure Agreement

One contract that you should strongly believe in and support is the nondisclosure agreement. If two companies are truly to become partners, candid, detailed conversations must take place. This is the only way to promote a better understanding of the goals of your company and the reasoning that went into certain decisions. A nondisclosure agreement sends a message certifying the seriousness of the discussions and plans for the future.

A properly executed agreement clearly spells out what types of information you will be sharing, what is of a sensitive nature from a competitive or technological perspective, and how the parties are to share and keep such information confidential. The agreement documents the life of the project, the parties involved, and how the information is to be controlled. It should also define common knowledge information, which cannot be held confidential. Thus, the responsibility for its dissemination cannot be determined, nor parties held accountable or at risk.

There are two benefits to executing this kind of agreement. The first is a clear attempt to protect your future marketing plans, designs, products, customer base, pricing information, and technology from competitive disclosure. The second benefit may be less obvious, but it is equally important. By asking a potential partner to execute such an agreement, you are making a commitment to bring that supplier into the inner confines of your business, to share the workings of your company, and, by implication, are making a strong gesture toward a future, long-term partnership.

Summary

As indicated, I have not attempted to present all the legal ramifications of a contract. Others can do that better than I can, and many books are out there to help you become more proficient in this area. Search out adequate and qualified legal counsel, where required. The costs will be offset by the savings of time and resources in trying to correct a poorly drawn agreement.

Instead, I am promoting the idea of placing partnerships ahead of contracts. I have discussed here (and in earlier chapters) the means to achieve these goals, including open communications, sharing of information, understanding your suppliers' point of view, and being mutually committed to future success. It is better to reduce the opportunities for parties to hide behind a stack of ink-stained paper when, by working together to solve problems, they are in a position to exploit unforeseen opportunities. Global sourcing in the twenty-first century must be based upon understanding and a strong handshake, and the moral commitment that entails.

CHAPTER 18

Negotiations

PERHAPS THE SINGLE MOST IMPORTANT MEASURE of success for a buyer will be his abilities as a negotiator. As Ronald M. Shapiro and Mark Jankowski said in their book, *The Power of Nice—How to Negotiate So Everyone Wins—Especially You,* "The best way to get what you want is to help the other side get what they want." The ability to negotiate is a skill set requiring training and experience, and it is one that a good buyer must use effectively on a daily basis.

Negotiation skills are becoming so critical that one could spend her entire career honing them, and still have room for improvement. With the global economy requiring an entirely new negotiation process and expectations, the caliber of skill sets has risen to a point not even perceived of twenty years ago.

It is difficult to do justice to the amount of preparation and work needed to become a skillful negotiator. Presented here are some overall hints and ideas on how to approach the topic, how to set goals and expectations for negotiations, and how to identify techniques to help in the process.

Win–Win Negotiations

In the past, negotiations were likened to war, and books were written using battlefield analogies and armies as metaphors for the negotiation process. Meetings were seen as confrontational tests, discussions that focused on opposing sides. Strategies were taught on how to win the battles, and ultimately, the war. Success was associated with the annihilation of your enemy, and to the victor went the spoils. Only one side was to leave the room under its own power. Clearly stated, one side of the negotiation process was expected to be the winner, one side, the loser. Negotiation was war.

That was wrong then, and it is wrong now. Think of a negotiation session under these circumstances, where price might be your main issue. Picture yourself as the leader of the successful bargaining team that achieved an unbelievable price concession from your opponent. Conquering hero that you are, you march proudly back to your company, surrounded by the good cheer of your colleagues and management. You won; your opposition lost.

But what is the more likely outcome of your win? You negotiated a great price for your company, but when the analysis was all done, your supplier, the conquered enemy, was left with no way to make a decent profit from your relationship. Your vendor took on your business and, now that the numbers are in, it has become painfully obvious that attaining it was no bargain.

ABC Widget Company's component is critical to your future, or you would not have spent so much time and effort in trying to get a good deal. But now that it knows it can't make any money doing business with you, how likely is the company to be a significant contributor to your success? How much influence do you think your pleading calls for parts to be delivered will have? How likely is it to make last-minute schedule changes, or to react to other conditions on your behalf? If ABC Widget Company can't make a reasonable profit by doing business with you, efforts on your behalf will be minimal.

In the end, you may have won the battle in the negotiation conference room, but lost the war when it came time to perform. In other words, Mr. Conquering Hero, you may have an incredible price, but what you don't have, and can't get, is product.

If both parties don't walk away from a negotiation as winners, then the process has failed. Negotiation results are either win-win, or lose-lose. There are no other possible outcomes.

Partnerships

Future business negotiations will be about building long-term relationships. Except for the rare circumstance where there is only a onetime requirement, most business associations will be forged with an
ongoing relationship in mind.

A good example is in trying to do business in the Far East. As you
will see in Chapter 20, most companies there are not interested in
the onetime order, but are willing to invest the time and energy to
build the structure that allows them to do business with you for many
years into the future. Companies and their key players typically are
interested in getting to know your company, business, markets, key
personnel, structure, and anything else that will help them understand who you are and where you are going. They want to get to
know the people they might deal with on a daily basis, to ensure they
understand you and your disposition.

It is only after this getting-to-know-you time that a company will
make a commitment for a long-term business relationship. As a
sourcing specialist, you should be taking the same approach with
your current and future vendors and suppliers.

This is a key point to keep in mind when setting a negotiation
strategy. Going in for the quick kill and instant gratification will be
at the expense of future opportunities. Taking every last bit of money
off the table today will be a very expensive proposition in the long
term.

Knowing the Needs of All Parties

Your job as a successful negotiator is to understand exactly what the
people across the table need from you. You must know what they are
looking for and what will address their requirements for the future.
Study this hard and be sure you have clear answers, to the point of
understanding them almost better than your own needs. Their goals
are rarely what they first claim them to be, not always what they
appear to be, almost always not what you first assume them to be,
and never the same as yours.

How do you go about doing this? It is not easy, but it can be fun
and will be rewarding. Before facing a crucial negotiation, research
the company. What is it doing that is new? Does it have updated

financial news out? Has it signed some new customers or contracts? Who are its major customers and competitors? Does it have new plants coming on line, a major personnel shift, and possible new strategic alliances on the horizon? What is the business press saying about the company and its products? Where does your company's product fit into its business for next year? What about the next five years?

Discover how critical you are to its future, to the company's expansion plans and corporate goals. This is crucial information in weighing how much influence you really hold. You must know how you are going to bring value to the table, for yourself and your partner, long before you get there.

As a successful negotiator, the breadth of knowledge and understanding you are required to have is extensive. In addition to the general understanding of the company noted above, you should have prepared extensively for the specific topics to be discussed. On pricing, for example, you should clearly understand, almost down to the penny, the cost of producing your product. If you don't absolutely know your vendor's costs of production, how can you ever know if you are getting a fair and equitable price, one that will meet both of your needs? The same will hold true for capacity, logistics, and lead time, among other topics.

Know Thyself

Second to knowing the needs of your partner is a full understanding of your needs. You must not assume that the needs of your partner reflect your own needs.

While your most critical need might concern price and delivery, the vendor's need might revolve around its association with a new market, such as yourself. Clearly the two sets of needs are different, and, if properly approached, have a high probability for a successful outcome in the negotiation process. Your need for lower price is something the vendor might easily concede in order to gain new market penetration.

By understanding the needs of both players, you are likely to create a strategy of success for both companies. The cornerstone lies in trading something of value, in order to obtain something of value.

Alternative Needs

Price might be on everybody's lips when you first sit down to map out your strategy for the upcoming negotiations. After some careful study to understand your partners, you might come away with the knowledge that, although price is important, the fact that your current supplier is across the country, and could expose your company to the risk of stock-outs and lost manufacturing time, is an issue to be addressed. If your proposed new partner is located in closer proximity, and is willing to stock inventory to ensure your never being out, then that might well be reflected in a lower total cost of doing business, something worth going after. What is clear in this example is that price is not your most important issue; product availability is.

Quality presumes a similar question. If the new partner can provide better, more consistent quality, limiting the amount of rejected materials to be handled and accounted for, then there is value in that, above pure purchase price.

Your true needs are reliable product availability, reduced raw material inventory, and better quality. Purchase price has now moved quite far down the list.

In modern times, alternative issues usually outstrip price as questions of paramount importance to be addressed. These might include technological issues, the total cost of procurement, willingness to work together on solving tomorrow's issues, strategic partnership capabilities, researching more efficient alternatives, suggestions for process improvements, and new product innovations. Over the long run, these are all far more important than mere purchase price.

Helpful Tools of Negotiation

Keep in mind the true purpose of going through the negotiation process in the first place. The shortsighted might see the need to attain a simplistic, quick win, or find a product that is key to the organization's future. Others might see it as a temporary association until something, or someone, better comes along. But in today's partnership-oriented business climate, is this realistic?

Picture yourself across the table from your vendor, working all the points of a tough, but honest, negotiation. You are looking for specific targets that you have carefully identified, and you know exactly what your vendor's needs and objectives are. You know almost all there is to know about its customer base and competitive situation, and have done a detailed cost analysis of its products. These are all critical steps to the process.

But unless there is something unique about the process you are involved in, the real need is to create a long-term business partnership that will prove mutually rewarding. Think of the company across the table as a close associate in the making, not the enemy. This must be the ultimate goal of your negotiation sessions. If you perceive the potential deal to be anything significantly different than this, you are negotiating with the wrong partner, or have the wrong outcome in mind.

There are a number of very basic techniques to carry in your arsenal of negotiating tools. None apply to every situation; each must be pulled out at the right time, and the rest saved for another day.

Many Americans working in the Far East for the first time in the 1970s had not done their homework, held a false sense of superiority, and didn't know how to conduct themselves when faced with the emerging Japanese giant. They expected to do business as they always had with a boisterous face-to-face confrontation, lots of pounding on the table, and a win-lose outcome. American businessmen arrived in Japan fully expecting to sit down at a conference table and, by the end of the day, stand up, deal in hand, conquerors once again.

Two weaknesses quickly became apparent to the negotiators sitting across from these brash Americans. The first was their desire for an instant deal. This was completely at odds with the Japanese approach of both parties getting to know those they were going to partner with. This meant regular social gatherings, dinners out together, and perhaps general meetings just to discuss issues of the day. It was only after such an investment of time that they would decide about doing business with the Americans. The seat of power had changed hands, and most American businessmen never saw it coming. In their headlong rush to get the deal done, the Americans usually gave away the farm.

The second weakness was the Americans' apparent abhorrence for silence, or dead airtime. While the Japanese contemplated the discussion and tried to grasp all that might have been said, the Americans were uncomfortable with the silence, and often stumbled in with more concessions or fewer demands, just to fill airtime. This weakness was exploited time after time by the Japanese negotiators.

The lesson here, regardless of the venue, is to not be afraid of silence; don't be on the lookout for airtime to fill. Always let your partner make the first move.

Another tool to remember is to never accept the first offer. When presented with it, you might look studious, appear to be considering it, or even look a bit disappointed, if you like, but first offers are rarely the best offer. Look for opportunities to expand the offer, or to find other things to throw into the pot. Don't be afraid to flinch at the second, or even third, offer. You know where you need to get to, and you know what the other party is capable of offering. Don't give up until you get comfortably close to that target.

Good Things Happen to Those Who Plan

There was an extended negotiation process in my past that I believe illustrates many of the points I've tried to raise. The team faced issues of understanding the needs of the potential supplier, how to feed those needs, knowing exactly what we wanted, Far East negotiating techniques, and arriving at a proposal that allowed everyone to leave the table a winner.

In the late 1980s, I was Materials Manager for the Entry Systems Division of Silicon Graphics, Incorporated, at the time an aggressive and rapidly growing manufacturer of powerful engineering work-stations.

Jim Clark, the founder of SGI, believed there was a huge, un-tapped market for a low-cost, desktop system. Technical performance was critical to the success of this project; low cost was another con-straint. Pennies counted. What we were attempting was to take a very high-priced, state-of-the-art technology, and make it available in a mass-produced desktop computer.

In relatively quick order, we were able to source the keyboard, monitor, and extended memory. The products that proved to be the most elusive and difficult to find were 350- and 700-megabyte SCSI disk drives.

We looked at several sources in the United States and overseas, finally settling on two possible suppliers, one domestic, one interna-tional. These were the only companies that either had announced, or were about to announce, having both products.

Over the course of several months, visits were made to the domestic manufacturer to see firsthand its capabilities. We checked business references, customer support, quality performance, technical skills, future growth, and new product plans.

The visit to Japan covered the same topics. A team from SGI spent a week there, visiting plants, holding technical discussions, drinking sake, and toasting each other over extended dinners.

Over the course of this process, we identified the negotiating needs of our potential partners as follows:

- ❑ The manufacturer in Japan needed to create a significant business relationship with a large U.S. customer.
- ❑ The domestic company had just purchased a competitive drive manufacturer, and needed a consistent customer for the additional capacity that came with the acquisition.
- ❑ Neither company believed it had a competitor in both products, and neither knew of the existence of the other during the negotiation process.
- ❑ Both companies were anxious to upgrade their image from a small supplier in the competitive and cutthroat personal computer supplier arena to a higher-grade supplier with better margins.

There were other issues of course, but what was germane to SGI and what we built our strategy on were the following:

- ❑ The issue to SGI was price and performance. This was far down on both vendors' needs lists.
- ❑ SGI desired one source for both products.
- ❑ Both suppliers were looking for credibility, better markets, and an association with a top-level customer.
- ❑ Both vendors needed entrees into new growth markets.
- ❑ One had significant excess capacity to fill.

SGI made the commitment that the drive manufacturer chosen would have every bit of our business, in both drives. We opened our books in terms of sharing forecasts, summary market analysis information, competitive analysis, and plans for new products.

In return, we expected a commitment for total support from the vendor, including dedicated warehouse inventory. We would have a first look at its new product innovations, and we would be on its design review committee to make future suggestions.

In the final agreement reached with the domestic supplier, we achieved all of our goals, as did the vendor. And, oh yes, we achieved a price commitment that exceeded our already aggressive price target, and one that an industry leader, purchasing approximately twice the number of units under more normal standard business practices, did not achieve.

Other Tools in Your Toolbox

There are several other tools to keep handy over the course of a negotiation process. A few simple ones to follow are listed below:

❑ Never make the first concession.
❑ Make your first concession a reasonable one.
❑ Make each subsequent concession smaller, less reasonable.
❑ Don't be afraid to ask the question. It may get answered.
❑ Find creative solutions.
❑ Recognize that good deals lead to more good deals.
❑ Know the terms.
❑ Keep written notes.
❑ Understand performance issues.

Summary

These are just a few ideas that you can work with during the course of your negotiation education. This chapter covers little more than the barest outline of items to consider or places to begin your negotiation training and skills. There are many good books on the topic, and many more seminars and training sites. Good skills can be learned, and a sourcing specialist must possess them.

The ability to negotiate effectively and fairly is one of the most important skills a good buyer will master.

CHAPTER 19

Partnership Is Not Just a Word

THE TERMS "PARTNER" AND "PARTNERSHIP" have become overused business mantras, their meanings diminished in the past decade. The concepts of partnership and partners grew alongside new production processes, such as JIT and Kan Ban, but, like many techniques imported and adjusted to fit the American manufacturing culture, lost some meaning in translation, and a great deal more in execution.

A Rose-Colored Vision

Like JIT, companies eager to improve their quality, customer service, and profitability during the early 1990s quickly adopted the terminology of partnership, without a clear understanding of the implications and commitments it entailed. Common wisdom dictated that a strong partnership with suppliers would allow a company to improve its processes, productivity, and quality, without much more than a handshake and a verbal commitment to a vague, touchy-feely notion of the latest business incantation.

The common misconception was that telling a supplier it was now your partner would become the magic elixir in your sourcing brew to help solve your internal ills. This new best friend would supply a better-quality product, at a reduced cost, and in less time than the old vendor did. The company would be there at a moment's notice to correct a problem, work all night to deliver product that you couldn't schedule properly, and would carry a variety of inventory, just in case you might need it.

The early failure of JIT was a result of the mistaken assumption that all issues revolving around delivery and poor planning could be pushed upstream to the supplier. The supplier would carry the inventory that you were unwilling to commit to, would have the entire product available at a moment's notice, and would have the ability to invest in all the raw materials that your company couldn't afford to.

Partnerships were a natural evolution of JIT, but the abuse worked the same way. All of the flexibility was forced upstream to the new partner, all of the risks locked in its stockroom instead of yours. In addition, the vendor was expected to attain efficiencies in its manufacturing process that you could only dream of. The final flash of shortcoming always came during a business cycle slowdown, when trusted partners were cast aside in favor of a slightly lower quote from a competitor hungry for business.

One-sided partnership commitments, based upon mistrust, miscommunication, and misunderstanding, failed miserably.

Partnership Defined

Partnerships are the only way that global business relationships are going to flourish and grow in the twenty-first century. The company unwilling, or unable, to develop strong, significant relationships with key suppliers and technology leaders will not prosper. Instead, it might easily decay, be consumed by competitors and conglomerates, or slowly choke to death on its own failed business plans.

Key companies will have created strong bonds with a critical few suppliers in their field. They will have joined forces to ensure mutual future success. In doing so, and in nurturing a growing relationship, critical suppliers will not have much in the way of available capacity to serve those companies slow to develop partnerships, or late in recognizing the need to do so.

For this reason, strategic partnerships are among the most important activities for a business in the new millennium. The importance of partnerships is verified by its being discussed in almost every manner, in almost every chapter of this book.

A successful partnership influences price, quality, delivery, margins, efficiency, cash flow, and investment. A strong partner in the role of supplier can be the most important key to a company's future growth and success, and it can contribute significantly to how efficiently and effectively a company runs its daily business.

Defining Your Requirements

Many of the keys to developing a strong partnership are mentioned in other chapters in this book. Below is a simple summation of these, along with a few other ideas and thoughts.

Know Your Product Needs

Research and study your company and determine the exact specifications of the product you need and are looking for. Know exactly what it is you need. In doing the research, you might determine that the original requirement might easily be replaced by something not apparent in the beginning. You might discover that the original quality specs were too tight or too loose. You must understand what your needs are, how the item is to be used, what its specifications should be, and all the other details that go into coming up with the final description of what you require. Until you know and understand this, you are unlikely to identify the proper partner to team up with.

Understand Your Support Expectations

What exactly are you expecting in terms of support? Do you foresee weekly visits from your supplier? Be honest, are these hand-holding sessions? Are you expecting technological innovations? Idea and market sharing? Design support? Don't be naive and underestimate your needs or expectations, or, through misplaced ego, overestimate your capabilities.

Understand the Inventory Investment Risk

What are you expecting in terms of inventory investment? Do you foresee your supplier taking all the risks associated with inventory?

How much of this service are you willing to pay for? What information and forecasts are you willing to share? How frequently? Are you willing to let your supplier into your database?

Technology Requirements

Are you in the market for the technological leader? Do you foresee the supplier coming to you regularly with new products and ideas for your business? What level of creativity are you expecting?

Be Ethical in All Dealings

The last step in this process is being ethical. Do not overinflate or underinflate your business prognosis, markets, competitive position, or performance criteria, including quality. The best way to ensure that you are in the market for the right partner is to be painfully honest and clear as to what your expectations and needs are from a vendor. Underestimating the true level of requirements is a very common error, and steps should be taken to lessen the chance of that occurring.

My practice is to clearly explain to potential new partners that, in our discussions, I will emphasize the weakness of our company over its strength. I will be open about the opportunities for improvement and areas that we need work on. I will explain our goals, and that we do have a process to get better, but we are not there yet. Finally, I explain that it is better to begin a relationship realizing that it might not be as bad as you might have believed, rather than finding it a great deal worse than you feared.

There are a number of ways to help ensure that you are beginning a relationship with a depth of awareness and reasonable expectations. One suggestion is to develop a questionnaire and checklist of critical points. It will be more accurate and honest if it has been freely circulated among all relevant departments in your company. This is not the time to allow inflated internal perceptions of your company to become stumbling blocks. Go into the process, like most successful relationships, with eyes wide open, expectations reasonable, and understanding where the muddy issues might lie.

The next step is reviewing your list of requirements and attempting to find the best match possible in a partner. Out of the research process your company had gone through, you should have a list of capabilities, refined to the point of delineating desired traits between the "gotta haves" and the "nice to haves."

What to Look for in a Partnership

Make sure you understand why you cannot attain every item on the first list, less on the second. In other words, a missing "gotta have" is much more important that a few or several missing "nice to haves." By following the steps below, you will more likely be able to winnow out a list of viable candidates, ones worth a second look in your search process.

- ❏ **Make a first pass at researching available companies and vendors.** You are looking for several key points, such as sales dollars, location, product availability, and support.
- ❏ **Weed out those vendors who are so large as to find your potential business insignificant to their daily lives.** By tying into a company that is too large, you will never get the level of attention you will occasionally require and never exert enough influence to prevent future problems.
- ❏ **Avoid the small company where you will become much more than about 20 percent to 25 percent of its business.** Although this vendor is likely to end up being a very responsive and supportive partner, its risks are too great, its future too closely tied to yours.
- ❏ **Schedule a face-to-face meeting.** Here you will ascertain the vendor's level of interest in your business and its potential commitment to your success. If, after a few initial discussions, you feel there is a level of commitment on the vendor's part, take a meeting to its site.
- ❏ **Visit the vendor's factories to ascertain capabilities, level of expertise, and commitment to your product or process.** How much floor space is dedicated to products such as yours? What are the unique manufacturing processes involved, if any? What is the level of efficiency? Quality standards? Operator training? Raw, work-in-process, and finished goods inventory levels? How well organized does it appear?

❏ **What is the vendor's customer base like?** How many of your competitors does it deal with? What are its sales order process, customer support, technical support, and willingness to work creatively with customers like? What are its financial terms for customers such as you? Is the vendor willing to extend special terms to gain your business? What does its financials look like?

❏ **Has the vendor asked you for your business?**

For further suggestions, refer back to Chapter 7.

At this point, you have done a lot of study, have asked a list of questions, and worked to understand the potential supplier's business and yours. Assuming that the questions are answered to your satisfaction, and you are pleased with the vendor's appearance and the results of your survey, then be ready to take the next step.

Now is the time to begin detailed discussions of your goals and expectations, what you are looking for in a long-term partnership, and your thoughts on a mutually beneficial business relationship. You must be willing to speak frankly, and share the information with your new partner.

I use an old analogy with regard to developing strong personal relationships. You must be prepared to open your kimono to a certain degree, if you expect your partner to do the same. Although you would never want to share every last secret, goal, or process at this stage, a frank, candid discussion will go a long way toward preventing future misunderstandings and fostering poor business decisions.

Vendor Responses

Creating a partnership is an involved, time-consuming process, and one not to be taken lightly. It is not unlike an extended negotiation.

Assure yourself that the vendor can supply your product, in the timing and quantities you require. You must know its quality capabilities and commitments, along with new technology offerings, if this is something that is important to you. Ask the most basic, most important question and then listen carefully for the answer, spoken and implied: Is the company interested in becoming your partner?

One of the keys to a successful negotiation outcome is listening.

Hear what is said and what is implied, filtering out your own expectations and preconceived assumptions. Only then will you be able to get a picture of where your potential partner is trying to lead you.

A Success Story

As discussed in Chapters 9 and 18, taking the extra steps to really study the needs of your vendor will pay off. At the same time, understanding your motives, what you must have, and where you can compromise will take you a long distance down the road to success.

This was the case in an exercise that my staff at one company worked through. A key supplier had been working with the company for many years, and was considered a high-quality, very responsive partner. It had worked on several new products during that time, and had made significant cost-reduction suggestions that were easily implemented.

The highest-volume product we purchased was a particular glue with a very strong market niche. It was universally received as a premium product, and able to sell into the marketplace at a higher price than its competitors.

Nevertheless, it was clear that the competition was beginning to nibble away at total volume of the product, and the reason was cost-driven. As part of the effort to address the issue, my company approached the vendor with a few alternatives, asking for its support in coming up with a new strategy.

Although the product was purchased complete in drums, and deliveries were scheduled from a manufacturing plant a few hours' drive away, the price we were paying was something that would have to be reduced if we were to remain competitive and maintain product volumes.

After very careful studies that incorporated planned factory efficiency improvements along with process changes, a target purchase price was arrived at. Although aggressive, our sourcing specialist believed it fair and equitable for both companies.

The vendor disagreed, and although it understood our situation, only offered a portion of what we required to meet our goal. We candidly explained that we understood its position, but because of pressing market demands we had no choice, and were being forced to pursue other alternatives.

We began to engineer the product to be manufactured in-house. After a prolonged period, we felt we had a workable recipe. At all times during this process, the current supplier was advised of our status, progress, and goals.

Discussions continued, and we remained very up-front and honest with all parties involved. The vendor knew it was a member of the team, and continued to review the process and made several valuable suggestions to help us out. Our partner also made an occasional price offer, which although attractive, still didn't quite meet our needs. We stayed the course in working toward our in-house manufacturing goal.

We reached the point where we had to make the decision to proceed, and commit the capital required to begin the conversion to an in-house process. We asked for one last meeting, where we presented our plans, current market conditions, and offered the last opportunity for the vendor to get on board. It was decision time.

We had worked hard to maintain a strong relationship throughout the process, and were up-front and aboveboard in all of our discussion on needs, market implications, and plans for moving forward.

At this time the vendor asked for some additional time, and requested two weeks to come back to us. We granted the request, making it very clear that this was the end of the line and we would be at decision-making time.

In the spirit of a strong partnership relationship, the vendor came forward with a completely new offer. One of its issues was transportation of the product to our plant. Its proposal included putting a bulk storage facility on-site, where ingredients could be delivered and stored as required, saving the vendor deliveries, and scheduling issues for my company.

In return for a long-term partnership agreement, it would lower the price to the level that we required. Hands were shaken, a contract was written and signed, and the total cost savings in product and capital investment no longer required was close to $300,000.

The vendor's need was to continue a long-term relationship with a customer that, although nowhere near its largest, had always been one of its better ones in terms of consistency of demand and regular payment history. Our need was for a steady stream of product at a reduced cost to reflect the changing market conditions facing us.

This is an excellent example of two partners working together, and although each faced differing needs, by coming to a mutually beneficial agreement, both ended up winners.

Summary

If you follow the steps outlined here, you will have clearly identified and understood the detailed specifications and expectations of your requirements. You will have carefully looked at alternatives, and settled on the final product.

The next step would be to do the research into possible partnership candidates, weeding out not only those obviously not qualified to support your needs, but also possibly the largest and smallest candidates, to ensure your getting the proper level of attention, while not putting an inordinate strain on the resources of your supplier.

You would then invite the final candidates to a detailed conversation to explore the feasibility of a long-term future business partnership. During the conversation, you will have determined the level of interest and commitment to the relationship from your candidate, the details of its process, and capability of supporting your total needs.

It is only after all of these steps are followed and all questions answered that you will be in a position to move toward closing a final partnership agreement. As one of the most important concepts in the arena of twenty-first-century sourcing, the need for strong partnerships cannot be emphasized enough.

CHAPTER 20

Wide World of Parts

AS SUPPLIERS AND CUSTOMERS, we are all part of a growing global economy. International business has expanded to the point where it is difficult today to find a product with only a single country of material content. Certain government and other contracts that require this may be difficult or impossible to fulfill in the not-too-distant future, as even domestic companies move key manufacturing and technological capabilities offshore.

This is an evolving process, especially from the sourcing side of the equation. In searching out the opportunities, a number of companies have recognized the need to go global. However, they have approached the process as a problem to be solved, instead of spending the time to create a proper sourcing strategy.

Other companies have not done a good job of recognizing the opportunities available in global, offshore sourcing, or they have failed to properly execute plans to procure product internationally.

The topic of offshore procurement is vast, and worth the effort to study and understand. By careful consideration of the process, creating a reasonable set of expectations, developing an appropriate plan and goal, and the steps required to get there, you will contribute toward putting your company in a position to reap important benefits.

International procurement covers a vast territory. For the purposes of this book, the focus is on the Far East, and China, specifically. Other areas of the world are noted for their own specialties, but when price and cost reduction are the issue, then the Far East is the address to look at, with China growing as the largest potential supplier of least-cost product.

Following the Lead of Lower Prices

During the late 1970s and early 1980s, Taiwan was an excellent market to shop for low price and good quality. The labor force was well educated and driven to succeed. The government maintained a tight grip on the labor supply, and strict wage controls were enforced, with an increase in benefits offered employees offset by a lowered primary wage.

Strategically located industrial parks were situated close to seaports and Chiang Kai-shek international airport. U.S. company names were blazoned across the front of many of these buildings, including General Motors, Xerox, and Ampex.

At the time, Hong Kong was also a recognized manufacturing leader, although even then it was known to be more expensive than Taiwan. However, this was offset by a recognized ability to produce a generally accepted higher quality of goods and supplies.

Singapore was already a high-tech location, and most of the advanced electronic and semiconductor companies were located there, making high-precision components.

At the time, China was still pretty much off-limits, with access strictly controlled. The leaders of the government that followed the reign of Mao Ze-dong (Mao Tse-tung) recognized the need to become a member of the world order. They knew one of the first orders of business was to create an international currency. Failure to successfully change the course of the sleeping giant would relegate China to the status of a backwater, agricultural country without a real role in the twenty-first century.

Things Have Changed

Labor was especially conservative in Taiwan and Hong Kong, and many individuals gave up the working life when investments in their countries' stock markets paid off, making many of them wealthy. Why work when you could live the good life in a culture where image was everything?

Today, the population of China is changing rapidly. With the growing liberation, factories have sprung up, and the country has become the next low-cost resource for world companies. Coolie hats and green uniforms are seen only at tourist traps. Mercedes, Buicks, and vans have replaced donkey carts and small trucks as vehicles of choice. Thousands of bicycles and scooters still flitter about, weaving in and out of traffic like bugs on a windy day. But they are competing for space on multilane highways and wide, thoroughfare-like central city streets.

A strong middle class is emerging, eager to become a part of the world order. This middle class recognizes the value of education and doing business with international partners. As factory managers, they will provide the right products to customers, while studying and learning the means to succeed and grow.

The Far East Personality

There is very little in the way of government-support programs in China. Welfare and unemployment compensation, as we know them, do not exist. There are some very minor payment programs available, most of which last a few weeks at most and pay next to nothing. All citizens are expected to find a way to make a living and survive. The consequences of not doing so are severe.

For this reason, business relationships are very important in China. The typical businessperson a Westerner might encounter operates with a different perspective and set of goals in mind. This is a critical lesson for all Westerners to learn and understand.

Relationships built there are intended to be strong and to last for a long time. The Far East businessperson is not interested in the one-order deal, or a relationship with a short life span. Instead, she is looking to build a long-term partnership to last for many years.

The second priority is that in China they believe in conducting business under a mutual benefit umbrella. The owner of a factory will first focus on keeping the money in the family, next in the neighborhood. What this means is that factory owners expect to pass some of the work from your business with them on to other family members, or to related companies.

This brings up the third issue—trusting your new partner. Because of these family relationships, there are some who consider this a reason to distrust your Chinese business counterparts. I disagree. As discussed in the chapter on negotiating, upon entering any business agreement, you must know all you can about your potential new partner. It is especially important in this situation. If you understand the vendor's expectations, and you investigate the relationships thoroughly, then this is just another part of doing business. Unless you see an overt conflict or reason not to do the business, then the deal should be acceptable, and you should be able to trust your new partner.

Another wonderful characteristic about the business relationships in China is the amount of up-front efforts companies will expend in learning your product and how to build it successfully. Companies will invest heavily in research and training, and in developing the tools and processes to make the business relationship a success. It is not unusual for a company to invest so much in process development as to not make a profit for upward of a year. This is part of why there is insistence on a long-term business agreement.

On subsequent visits to supplier factories, you will likely be surprised at the creative solutions presented. Don't look for heavy investments in machine tools, but do look for innovative applications of simple processes and equipment. Remember, people are clamoring for employment, and labor is cheap there, so there are no benefits to be realized from labor-saving equipment.

Barriers to Success—Real and Imagined

We have addressed some of the past weaknesses that American businesspeople tend to exhibit when negotiating in the Far East. There are other obvious barriers to bringing a potential deal to fruition, such as language and backgrounds, lack of common principles and expectations, and misunderstanding of body language and physical movements.

The Chinese civilization and culture is many thousands of years old. We Americans have a history of just over two hundred years. Chinese history is rich in old traditions and ways of dealing with each other. I am in no position to judge their ways or culture. As a sourcing person dealing with them, neither are you. The Chinese are a very proud people, although outwardly humble. Keep that in mind and deal with them by exhibiting respect and honor for their customs.

Just as it failed in Japan in the 1970s, the typical American in-your-face approach to negotiations will not work in China. A case in point occurred on a recent visit. When presented with a particular product to consider, I was embarrassed to hear a colleague at one meeting respond with, "That's junk, and no one is interested in it."

"That's very interesting and something we might want to look at in the future," would have been the better response.

I won't cover some of the giveaways that have already been discussed, but do keep this in mind. Typically, Chinese people are very competitive and tough in a negotiation, and they are not easily rolled over to an American preconceived notion. They hold their ground, are quite firm, and sometimes, indelicate to American ears. Keep in mind your needs and expectations, and above all, be patient. Chinese businesspeople will often use bluster in situations they might not clearly understand.

In meeting with the Chinese, take the time to read the body language. Often it is telling you much more than the spoken words. Yes does not always mean yes, and no does not always mean no. The people are exceedingly polite, and vagueness on their part may well be a desperate effort to save face or prevent embarrassment, usually yours.

Unless your company is willing to spend heavily and completely in a facility in China, do not expect a small investment, say 20 percent of the business, to yield you the same influence that it might with a domestic company. The corporate laws are lax at best, confusing at worst, and in the end, who and where would you sue, and how would you prove it?

It is safe and fair to expect a long-term, productive, and beneficial relationship to develop in China. As with anything else, you must do your homework.

A Few Rules to Prosper By

Here are some rules to keep in mind when considering doing business with offshore suppliers.

❑ **Don't send new technology to the Far East unless you want to see it available everywhere and from many suppliers.** China has no real copyright and trademark laws, and patents are little more than a receipt for monies sent to a central patent government office. They have no legal effect. The World Trade Organization is struggling with this issue. If they can't find a quick, effective solution, there is no reason to believe you can.

❑ **Clearly define your goals and expectations from your offshore source.** It is much more effective to provide very specific written plans, specifications, and goals than to assume that everyone understands everything that was said or implied. You are dealing with cultural, language, intellectual, and legal barriers, on both sides of the table. Assume nothing, verify everything. Ask the critical questions several different times and in several different ways.

❑ **Wherever possible, avoid brokers and trading companies.** Find the actual manufacturer of the product you are interested in. Deal directly with that company. If you must begin the process through a middleman, before the first product is shipped to you, make arrangements to visit the factory to check your goods firsthand.

❑ **Verify the working conditions in the factory.** Not only must you conduct an on-site visit to validate that your partner can make the product and meet your needs, you must be on the lookout for issues that should be ethical deal breakers. Although not as widespread as it once was, be watchful for child labor, poor lighting, and ventilation. Check for adequate restroom facilities, and verify there is plenty of drinking and washing water available. The Chinese as a culture are a close people and used to sitting next to each other. Just be sure the conditions are reasonable. Check for machine noise levels, safety controls on equipment, open containers of chemicals, and materials not carefully stored or handled. Look at the general housekeeping in the factory; is it clean and organized, or is trash and waste scattered all about?

❑ **Find an honest, reliable freight forwarder.** Freight handling can be notoriously illogical and inefficient at best, rife with graft and kickbacks at worst.

❑ **Plan on several site visits over the course of your business.** This will serve as a firsthand check on actual progress and implementation of your expectations. Also, nothing improves and strengthens a business relationship like face-to-face meetings. Most offshore companies really want to make long-term business plans, and require a personal relationship.

Summary

In China, opportunities for future success from the sourcing point of view are limited only by your imagination. This is a vast, new, and emerging capitalistic power that will prove to be a significant resource for a long time to come. Regardless of the migrations of Far East resources in the past, the difference is that China will remain a force for a long time to come based on the sheer size and population of the country.

Just as important, China needs political and financial capital to become a world player. If it is going to become the trading partner it desires to be, China is going to have to continue making strides on the world front. "Beijingers, friends to the world," the country's 2008 Olympic motto, is not an accident.

The sourcing specialist, and the functions willing to travel to the country and gain the knowledge required to be a success, will be amply rewarded for a number of years to come.

CHAPTER 21

It's Your Career

AS WE ALREADY KNOW, most successful sourcing specialists began their careers in lower-level positions, working their way up with time and experience. Under the current nomenclature, a new person might begin her career as a junior, nonexempt buyer responsible for MRO or office supply buys. With the appropriate seasoning and training, she might progress to a sourcing position, gradually taking on more responsibility and authority with accumulated experience. A senior sourcing specialist will usually have five to ten or more years of experience in the procurement area.

Skill Sets

The first trait that every sourcing specialist needs to cultivate is the willingness (and ability) to think creatively. The logical, but wrong, assumption is that a good sourcing specialist is not a creative personality. Coming up with a unique solution to a problem is a key to success in the new sourcing arena. Old methods of doing business, the same tired solution set, and the tunnel vision of being ruled by contracts or other written documents when looking at conflicts and opportunities will not work in today's business environment. Creative problem solvers will be sought out for a long time to come in sourcing.

The ability to see beyond the obvious, to look around corners for an elusive solution to a problem or a unique approach to achieving success, is the level of creativity required. Sometimes this skill set will manifest itself in a unique phrase within the terms-and-conditions of an order or purchase agreement that will help solve a problem and assure success. At other times, it manifests itself in a clear understanding of the true needs of a potential vendor partner and finding a way to meet them. An open mind is a great asset that should be cultivated.

At the same time, thorough attention to detail is required. It is important that a subtle clause or turn of a phrase in a purchase agreement does not present an undue risk to your company. The sourcing specialist is the first line of defense in preventing this from occurring. This attention to details also applies to the pricing and quantity information, schedules, packing size, and mode of transportation, all possible impediments to success. As should be apparent by now, the bandwidth of the sourcing thought process ranges from the grand overview down to the minutiae.

Perseverance is another key trait of the successful sourcing specialist. Over the course of a long negotiation or detailed system implementation, it is easy to mentally relax your grip, to give up on the little issues, in the hopes of bringing a project to a conclusion.

It is only through perseverance that the final success will be achieved. Sourcing specialists who can stick to their goals, and dig in more as the project gets tougher, are the ones that become the stars of the team.

Be cautious, however, because perseverance by and of itself is also a weakness. For example, single-mindedness that prevents a sourcing specialist from being open, or from grasping the potential for a new idea, can lead to a misstep. The valuable sourcing person quickly grasps an opportunity that might be present in a new idea, no matter in whose mind it may have germinated and taken life, and he is willing to adopt it and nurse it through to implementation.

Stepping Stones Along Your Career Path

Clearly, you are reading this book because you are interested in sourcing. It is likely you are, at the least, a new buyer or a newly promoted buyer. If you are a company manager or owner, the points presented are also of interest to you. Perhaps they are serving as guidelines for creating a new sourcing direction within your company. Or, these points might serve as idea generators for how to assess or set goals for your employees. The important thing to keep in mind is that the chapters present in this work only skim the surface of each topic. To be considered a complete sourcing specialist, you have to mine the depth of knowledge below the surface.

Seminars are another excellent avenue of training. There is nothing like hearing a fellow sourcing specialist speak to a topic on which he is knowledgeable and passionate. More than a textbook, a class or seminar allows for the human interaction of questions, comments, and answers that are not available within the confines of a book, or on a video screen.

Seminars are also a wonderful venue for meeting other people in the same kind of work, people who face many of the same kinds of day-to-day problems and issues. Not only do you want to bring a notebook to a seminar, you also want to be sure to have a stack of business cards available for trading with classmates. Make the effort to greet as many people as you can, and exchange cards. This is also a great way to build up a personal network of people who can be called on if the need arises.

Don't overlook the professional associations. APICS, formerly the American Production and Inventory Control Society, has a focus on production control, forecasting, and inventory management. It is a great organization to join if you are interested in understanding what drives some of the requirements of your daily job.

The Institute for Supply Management (ISM), formerly the National Association of Purchasing Management, is a professional organization of purchasing and sourcing specialists. Monthly magazines, local members and chapters holding regular meetings, a variety of books and literature on the subject, and an industry-recognized certification process are all available through ISM.

The reference section at the end of the book lists additional professional associations, along with a few training organizations to improve your purchasing and quality understanding and skills. It, too, is an incomplete list.

Another local source of knowledge can be easily overlooked. These are the fellow employees in your own company. As you climb the ladder of experience, ask yourself if there is a more senior person who really impresses you with her apparent knowledge or skill. What about your supervisor or boss? A department manager who has been with the company for a long time? These people earned their current positions by acquiring a great deal of experience and job knowledge, and they likely would be happy to share their backgrounds with you as mentors.

Ask if they would participate in regular meetings or roundtables with others in the department to discuss problems, opportunities, or past experiences that might serve as good training examples. Would they be willing to help guide you in the steps it takes to attain your goals? There might be opportunities to sit in on higher-level meetings or negotiations as an observer to see firsthand how the process works.

Want an easy-to-follow recipe for success? Read. Read the business trade papers and periodicals. Read the textbooks and other business books. Look into articles on the Internet. Even advertising literature can offer something of value or an insight as to how something works. All businesses are intertwined in some manner, and all do similar kinds of work in a variety of ways. The more you study and learn, the more value you bring to the job. The more ideas you learn and apply to your position, the more valuable you become to your organization.

Measuring Progress

In some ways it is difficult to quantify the progress made by an employee over time. Speaking as a manager of a successful sourcing department, I know that, unless I keep little records and notes, it is easy to lose track of the accomplishments of individual members of my staff.

In the end, it is your career. You are the person ultimately responsible for your success. You cannot assume that others are always watching out for your best interests, no matter how good their intentions. Be able to remind your manager about that great cost saving you achieved, or the way you recovered from a critical vendor's stopping deliveries.

I had an employee who regularly reported that she "did stuff and made things happen," when I asked her for progress updates. I knew she was a hardworking, efficient, and very productive employee, one of the strongest on my staff.

Even so, when it came to review time, I had difficulty recalling several significant accomplishments she had made over the previous year. She felt she had little time to accumulate her accomplishments. But if not her, who? Like any successful employee, she couldn't afford not to keep me informed of her achievements.

Not wanting to document your own successes is a false modesty that could prove detrimental to your career. Instead, maintain an "I love me" file. It can exist in a drawer, a folder, even a file on your computer. No matter the location, drop yourself little notes of accomplishments, cost savings, tips you've learned, even periodic successes and how you achieved them.

At the end of a few months, you will be pleasantly surprised to discover just how much you've learned, how much you've accomplished, and most important, how far you have progressed. In the meantime, you will have an accurate record when the boss asks, "What have you done for me lately?"

Two More Examples

Cost savings are so important today that many larger companies are setting multibillion-dollar cost-reduction targets, directives in most cases, to be achieved by their sourcing departments. The numbers are so important, and the total profit-and-loss contribution of the sourcing groups so critical to success, that they receive top management attention.

If finance is the reporting arm when calculating the numbers, then there is an objective party overseeing the process, which lends credibility to the results. For a smaller company, this might be cumbersome, so an easy way is to calculate the annual reduction based upon the forecasted demand at the time the first lower-cost units, or process, is utilized.

Another point is to be sure to track your history of increasing responsibility. You might find that, although you started two years ago purchasing office supplies, today you are solely responsible for all chemical buys for the company, an annual purchase in the millions of dollars, and a key area of responsibility to the manufacturing plan.

Good performers have a tendency to take on more tasks without realizing it, and managers have a willingness to send the work to the person most likely to succeed. Document each new assignment, each new success.

Note, also, key negotiations you participated in or led, and the strategies pursued. Why were they successful or what was missing that caused them to fail?

Every activity that the sourcing specialist becomes involved with incurs something learned along the way. Every milestone is a track record of your progress and success.

Summary

In the end, it's your career, and the only party responsible for your growth and success is you. The company may, or may not, have a vested interest in your success, or, more particularly, in your growth. If you truly are interested in growing into new career responsibilities, and are passionate about your own success, then you are the one responsible for making it happen.

Take the initiative in steering your career, and in taking the right steps for success. Learn everything you can about all aspects of the job. Take courses, read books and magazines, ask others for help, network, and join professional organizations.

Don't be corralled by false modesty. Periodically remind your boss of recent accomplishments and successes. Remind her how well you took on the latest task and how smoothly it is running now. Don't wait for others to give you the recognition you feel you've earned. Go out and get it.

CHAPTER 22

It's a Question of Ethics

AS I AM WORKING ON THIS BOOK, the front pages of every newspaper in the country are awash with the sordid details of how yet another corporation is being investigated for financial and business reporting irregularities. The list is made up of not only young, upstart companies whose behavior might be, if not excused, at least explained by the exuberance and inexperience of youth, but instead, includes many companies that might, at one time, have been considered role models for exemplary corporate behavior.

It would be easy to conclude that business in America has lost its ethical and moral rudder when, in addition to Global Crossing, Adelphi Communications, WorldCom, and Enron, long-respected names such as Xerox, Merck, and Bristol-Myers Squibb are also under investigation. All companies must be presumed to be innocent until proven otherwise, but their being in the shadows of suspicion does not portend well for the perceived level of honesty in the business community.

The moral and ethical questions facing the country today are not limited to corporations. The marbled halls of Washington are included, and politicians in Congress are being pulled into the fray. The most recent example, Representative James Traficant of Ohio, was

175

forced out of the chamber by his colleagues only days before being arrested and jailed.

Nor does the questionable behavior end with Congress. Questions of ethics and corporate malfeasance are even being asked at the top levels in the White House.

Concentrated Responsibility

In the sourcing world, organizations are lean, and the buyer's role is one of enhanced decision-making capability and control. The members of this team are expected to be consummate professionals, assuming the role of responsible staff controlling a significant portion of the cash assets of a company. A signature on a document, an electronically transmitted order, or a blanket schedule might authorize the spending of hundreds of thousands of company dollars. The integrity inherent in that signature must be above question and reproach.

The span of responsibility extends well beyond the money involved in the placing of an order. The sourcing specialist of today is a key player in identifying and making recommendations who the supplier for an item should be. She is a key team member in deciding the final terms and conditions of doing business together, what the lot sizes will be, transportation arrangements, final specifications, and quality expectations, among other issues. These are all areas that entail considerable investment in time and money, and they all contribute in no small manner to a company's overall competitive position.

This is an unprecedented level of authority and responsibility residing on the desk of a single or limited number of buyers. The perceived methodology of decision making and the dollar spend must be unquestioned.

The Front Page

An old adage talks about never doing anything you would not be proud to have your family read on the front page of the local newspaper. When it comes to being a sourcing specialist, this is good advice. Take it.

I often train new employees using a very simple example to illustrate my expectations when it comes to honesty and integrity within a sourcing organization.

"Anyone can question my abilities," I begin. "They can question my thought processes, heritage, intelligence quotient, or perception. They can cast aspersions on my skill levels, experience, or understanding of company processes or goals. What I never want anyone to question is my integrity and honesty."

If you are in sourcing long enough, you will be exposed to opportunities that will test your integrity compass, your moral fortitude. I couldn't begin to list all the possibilities, but some popular ones are tickets to sporting or theatrical events, special gifts and incentives, trips, and less frequently now but still out there, good, old-fashioned cash.

The trap of rationalizing questionable behavior is an easy one to fall into. As a hard-working sourcing specialist, you easily could believe that vendor gifts and givebacks are earned perks, part of the job, a minor benefit rewarding your diligent efforts.

It is also possible to become friendly with certain vendors, perhaps meeting regularly after work for a casual glass of wine or dinner. This might become easier to justify with time because you have grown to genuinely like the sales representative and feel that you have a bond beyond the office and world of business.

Rationalizing questionable behavior usually occurs one small step at a time, leading down a dangerous and dark path. The consequences of this error are cumulative and can be devastating.

Appearances Are Everything

When it comes to business behavior, and this is true in areas well beyond the boundaries of sourcing, appearances become fact, and truth can be relegated to second place, if taken into account at all. When there is the appearance of equivocal behavior, or the opportunity for others to question your performance when it comes to vendors and your position, you have already lost. It's that plain and simple.

How do you go about protecting your reputation, and preventing yourself from being put in a position where your actions might be suspect? Think carefully about everything you do connected with your position.

A favorite hot button with many of your fellow employees will be lunches and dinners with suppliers. When the question arises, proper counsel should be that there is very little justification, particularly with a local supplier, to schedule lunch or dinner at a local bistro. The fact is that restaurants are not conducive to effective business meetings. They are noisy and distracting, certainly not secure, and no place to be dealing with difficult issues or delicate business topics. Any deal or activity accomplished over the course of a one or two-hour lunch most likely would have been successfully concluded in a shorter time span, and with less distraction, in an office or conference room.

Another favorite is theater or sporting event tickets. Sometimes vendors maintain a group of seats or a skybox at certain venues expressly to entertain clients and customers. At other times, they might show up at your front door, fistful of tickets in hand. At one company I worked at several years back, an electronics vendor arrived with pairs of very hard-to-get San Francisco 49er football tickets for every employee in purchasing, including clerical personnel.

The range of possible gifts is almost endless, and I have seen everything, including gift certificates from large department and catalog stores, automobile service, weekend trips, vacation discounts, and cases of wine or liquor.

Questionable Circumstances

There are a few, face-saving ways to deal with vendor-provided gifts and benefits, and I am not saying that every gift has an ulterior motive associated with it. I am only suggesting that if it appears that your decisions as a sourcing specialist could have been unduly influenced, if there is a level of doubt sufficient to create questions in your company peers and associates' minds as to your motives, then you have limited your boundaries and effectiveness.

Below are a few common situations, and how you might deal with them.

Restaurants

As indicated earlier, there are few instances where effective business can be conducted over lunch or dinner at a commercial establishment that could not be better handled in an office or conference room. Therefore, the general response might be to routinely decline all invitations. If not already in place, this policy will set a precedent that your company, peers, and suppliers will quickly come to understand and accept.

Occasionally a vendor will travel quite some distance to meet with you, and the meeting extends over a lunch period. If the situation dictates that a working lunch over sandwiches brought in might not be adequate, nor show the proper respect, then accept the prospect of going to lunch together. The caveat is that, as host, your company should always pick up the tab.

Tickets

The stock answer is never accept tickets of any kind. No matter how innocent, no matter how the event may or may not be related to work, there is still the appearance of receiving something of value that might be considered an influence.

Personal Items of Value

The same rules apply here as for tickets. Don't accept specialized pens, daybooks, auto services, or other items of a personal nature. A simple, but effective, rule is that nothing along these lines can be accepted unless it is of very minimal value and has supplier advertising prominently displayed. Under this definition, acceptable items might be a pad of sticky notes or a cheap ballpoint pen that has the supplier's advertising. An expensive set of writing instruments or a personally engraved date book are not.

Money

Cash and monetary equivalents are never acceptable, no excuse and no exceptions. A case for illegal kickbacks is more easily made with evidence of cash or financial incentives than any other commodity. As a manager, I would have serious reservations about the long-term prospects of anyone in my employ who accepted cash or monetary rewards, for any reason, from any supplier, potential supplier, or anyone else associated or attempting to do business with my company.

This is a very serious situation, and if someone offers you cash or other monetary rewards, associated or not with an action on your part, decline it instantly and emphatically, report it to your superiors, and follow it up in writing. Go on record with this kind of activity.

It should be clear that gifts provided members of the sourcing department of any kind, and for any reason, should be immediately and clearly turned down.

Ask yourself how you would have dealt with the 49er football ticket situation. Consider that the tickets were already in hand, the employees were happy to have them, and, as an ethical sourcing person, certainly might risk your associate-of-the-year award if you fumble. What would you have done as a sourcing specialist? Sourcing manager? Group manager? What paths might you take in this situation?

The way in which I dealt with it was head-on. I directed the purchasing manager to gather up all of the tickets, and to personally account for every one. I then called the president of the providing company, apologized for the apparent confusion, and asked that he send someone immediately to our company to pick up the tickets. I carefully explained our company and purchasing department policy of not accepting gifts, that I was sure this was just an oversight on his part, and that I was confident we would not be having this kind of conversation again.

We never did.

Other Integrity Risks

There are less obvious internal company issues that can raise ethical and integrity questions, and even though outside the vendor influence arena, they too, should be avoided.

No one person, including a sourcing manager or business team leader, should ever have access to both sides of a transaction. For example, systems should be in place so that the person who originates a purchase order with a vendor does not have access to, and cannot do, the receiving transaction or approve payment. There must be a solid wall between the two sides of any transactions that are monetary in nature.

A new vendor should be approved by at least two persons, in separate departments, before being loaded into the company database as an accepted supplier. In most cases, the requestor can be anyone in the company, and that sourcing can approve, with the final audit being in the finance department.

I mentioned earlier that dollar signature approval levels and controls for normal, inventory, or production items are a nonvalue-added activity. The same is not true for noninventory orders. Signature levels need to be carefully controlled and adhered to. Inventory items are received and stored by random personnel, locked up in a warehouse, and regularly cycle-counted, making abusive transactions more difficult to complete. Items not going into a reportable inventory account and more likely controlled by a single individual are also the ones most easily lost in the daily business shuffle. In the interest of control and separation of powers, at least two people should review a high-value requisition. Although a person might have a given dollar level of signature authority to originate the requisition, a person in sourcing should countersign the order showing he reviewed the requisition for proper account number and dollar-level signature approval. A third, independent person must do the receiving transaction.

Keeping a Secret

We have spent most of our time discussing ethics and honesty from the receiving side, the one that tends to get the most attention. When we discuss improprieties in human behavior, it seems the most ink is spilled on that side of the equation.

For the sourcing specialist, there is another area that he needs to be particularly sensitive to, and that is the sharing of confidential, nonpublic information he is privy to. In our daily dealings with design engineers, marketing planners, new suppliers, and vendors, it is easy to collect a great deal of information. The data could include new products coming to market from a known supplier, or a new, evolving market that has been identified, one not previously addressed. The information could be of a financial nature, and directed at a supplier or one of its competitors, or a specific or emerging customer.

Competitive quote information (including performance, as well as financial data) is another example. During the process of quoting, it would be normal to obtain specific pricing information from each competitor, along with any unique plans or creative ways in how they will serve your needs. In reviewing this information, you might see a solution to a long-running problem, and something you would like all competitors to address.

Sharing of any of this information, in any form, is not ethical. The information given you by each supplier is expected to be held and must be held in the strictest of confidence. This includes any plans or creative ways to service your account put forth by a bidder, along with specific dollar quotes.

Bid It Once, Bid It Right

Nor is it ethical to advise a bidder during the process the exact number or goal you are looking for, competitive bid information, or even who its competitors might be. It is partially for this reason that, during a bid process, you must firmly lay the groundwork and make it crystal clear that there is only one round in the bid process. Make it clear to the vendor that the first bid should be the correct one, as there will not be a second chance. It is too easy for a vendor to explain that she thought there would be more give and take, thus she did not bid her best offer on the first round.

The room for final negotiations and working out the specifics of the plan are during the groundwork phase, when you are supplying the bid package to all parties. At this point, ask that all parties contact you with any questions or items not clearly understood. Once there is an acceptance of the specifications and the ground rules, then all dancing around must stop. The serious business of quoting must begin.

If one of your bidders does the job right and gives his best estimates to meet your needs, is it fair or ethical that another bidder be given the opportunity to match or better those bids? Never tell a bidder until the results are finalized where its bid is, a percentage high or low, or what the price has to be.

The secret to a successful bid process, and ensuring that there are no questions of ethics or honesty in play, is to follow these directions. The only way to maintain an open and honest bid is to ensure that everyone is playing on a level playing field. The only way to do everything possible to attain this goal is to make sure the same rules apply to every player.

Overall Philosophy

If a gift or incentive is not provided to everyone in the company, then you are in a position to properly decline it. This basic philosophy is simple in concept, and makes it clear for the sourcing specialist when faced with a questionable situation in which she is not sure of the proper action.

There are no special rights associated with being a member of the sourcing team, and you should not expect any. You are paid and recognized by your company to do a certain job, just as every other employee is expected to do his job. You have a moral and ethical responsibility to your company to do the best job you possibly can, with no additional rights or privileges associated with that assignment.

Earlier, I alluded to certain situations where a gift did not necessarily have to be turned down directly. One company I know used a unique approach to the entire gift-giving process. When offered a gift of value, the required response was to advise the giver that company policy forbade accepting gifts of any kind. However, if the supplier had no objections, and it must always be provided the choice, the gift would be turned over to the human resources department. At subsequent companywide events, such as the summer picnic or winter party, the accumulated gifts were given to the employees as door prizes. The company also improved goodwill and publicly acknowledged each prize donor. This was a fair and equitable solution to all.

Summary

If there is to be a thumbnail rule for ethics and accepting gratuities from outsiders, it might be this: Don't. Decline with a polite thank you, or begin an accumulation program in your company for prizes, as illustrated above. The majority of people going to work every day are honest, hardworking, and desirous of doing a good job. Integrity is second nature to them. Build on this, and don't disappoint them by your bad example.

It would be a shame to bring into question your motives or integrity for the sake of a small gift or a few dollars. It would be even more of a loss to have your actions questioned because of a small misstep, with your never having actually done anything wrong, or unethical. It is for this reason, the risk of adverse appearances, that I emphasize the proactive approach of never bringing your activities or motives into question in the first place.

Unfortunately, and often unfairly, appearances are everything. Never allow a false witness to be your undoing.

Managing the Sourcing Department of the Future

IF YOU ARE THE VICE PRESIDENT of logistics or the director of materials of a modern, up-to-date company, you have invested a significant amount of time, effort, and capital to put together the sourcing team of the future. A few years back, you recognized the need and the change in the wind, did your homework, and spent time reading and researching the future of business in your product line. It became apparent that the globalization of business was going to be responsible for previously unheard of changes, not only in your processes, but also in your competition and customer base.

You took the time required to study the past and developed a vision of the future. You realized that past successes were then, and the same processes today will lead to failure. You have taken the steps to change the culture in your business, but you continue to question whether you have done enough, whether your have covered all the bases.

"If you have to ask the question, the answer is probably no," is the wrong school of thought. It is more important that you understand that change is evolutionary in nature, and thus is never complete. Instead of searching for the final answer, the one set of ingredients that will guarantee future growth, it is more important to be open to new steps. Understand that a complete list of required steps to success does not exist.

New Expectations

The sourcing department of the new century is made up of a group of specialists focused on a different vision than in times past. Purchasing departments of old consisted of paper-pushing administrators who placed orders based upon a specific need dropped on their desk by another administrator farther upstream. What they created was a single step in a long trail of paper steps. This is not the case today.

Today's sourcing specialist is a project manager, charged with creating, managing, measuring, and bringing to closure a series of larger tasks. She is not a buyer in the classical sense of the word, and she is certainly a far cry from the buyer described above.

Instead, the sourcing specialist must possess the imagination to see the future, and be trained in the intricacies of implementing a winning strategy for her company. As part of the execution of her vision, she will bring a team of functions together on a project, set goals and targets, report accomplishments, and measure the results. Depending upon the situation at hand, representatives from engineering, marketing, product design, sales, manufacturing, or finance may well be working on one of these projects.

A key member of the project team is the selected vendor, providing the necessary input, technical data, and process specifications to meet the required cost and performance goals. In times past, the supplier was identified at the end of the investigation. Today, the vendor is brought in at the earliest stages of the project. A modern sourcing specialist must recognize her company's unique set of support requirements and constantly search for opportunities to partner up with a source possessing matching capabilities. This is a far cry and a millennium away from the days of placing a purchase order in response to a requisition.

Support the Players, Not the Rulebook

This book has discussed in great detail how the old purchasing department processes no longer work, and how the roles of the sourcing specialist are changing, entering new venues not previously considered. As a manager, you must accept that your role is not exempt from the same forces of change. For these reasons, current processes, measurements, and controls might well be out of touch, and might, in fact, be hindrances to the last, vital steps to success. Frankly put, be sure you and your directives are not standing in the way of progress.

If the specialist is successful in creating a unique, new business relationship with a supplier, clearly the process of scheduling and handling product and correspondence will have changed. Correctly managed, a new sourcing project might put several items and a large volume of product under one sourcing umbrella. The management span of control will have changed with the elimination of several suppliers along the way. The sourcing specialist may have worked with the vendor to completely manage inventories, including daily delivery of requirements direct to your factory floor, necessitating a change in the material handling process.

It then stands to reason that the old mode of placing a specific purchase order, with a given line for a given item number, quantity, and date of delivery, is now cumbersome at best, at worst a hindrance and house of paper about to collapse in on itself. This kind of management control must be abdicated and eliminated, recognized as inefficient, costly, and counter to the new sourcing strategies.

We have talked about several techniques to replace this process, including more sophisticated Kan Ban techniques, more frequent deliveries, and smaller lot sizes. The benefits are reduced risks of obsolescence, improved quality, and reduced inventory investments. Indirect benefits also accrue to your organization in the form of the reduced costs of managing the paperwork.

Look Inward

As an astute manager, there are two areas here that you must carefully cultivate by encouraging your staff to think creatively.

First, be sure that the back-office processes in your company do not eat up your cost savings. Direct material savings must be matched by process and efficiency improvements made throughout the company. Hiring an army of paperwork clerks to support daily deliveries is not an acceptable solution.

Second, your role is to not expect a win with every project, but to accept the risk of failure as a key step along the path of improvement. The successful managers in this century's sourcing world will encourage creative efforts, recognizing and rewarding failures as attempts at pushing the boundaries of success. As a manager, you must provide the working environment and support to encourage your staff to be looking at the business through a new set of glasses. It is your responsibility to recognize the need for change and to support the efforts of your people actively working to define and implement these changes.

If the process is broken, don't hesitate to fix it. Your sourcing team will have identified several projects that warrant serious study. Properly executed, they will have researched all of the information, found the relevant data, deleted old beliefs and perceived knowledge from the equation, and arrived at one or more recommendations to improve a process, change a product, improve quality, or reduce costs.

How to Kill Innovation

Unfortunately for the lesser-managed company, it is often at this point that the process breaks down, snatching defeat from the salivating jaws of victory. A sure indicator is a discouraged sourcing department that has gone all this way in the process, only to be stymied by a bureaucracy perceived to exist solely to kill fresh thinking and innovation. Clear symptoms include a mountain of redundant paperwork, multiple levels of required signatures, endless meetings, fear of change, and comfort with the status quo.

Another effective killer of innovation and creative thinking is the "we've tried that before" syndrome. Sometime in the past, something similar may have been attempted and didn't succeed. Upon further investigation, it too often becomes clear that the idea wasn't actually tried, only discussed in great detail and killed by the company's team of entrenched devil's advocates.

The wise manager has two courses of action when faced with this form of resistance. The easiest is to acknowledge past efforts, making no comment on the outcome. Instead, emphasize that obviously the idea was ahead of its time, and it wasn't exactly the same as what is currently being proposed. Point out that there is a new team in place now, possessing a renewed sense of urgency that demands results.

The second step occurs after the naysayers have had adequate time to climb on board, but never quite managed to take the leap of faith. Negative attitudes quickly work their adverse magic upon even the most inspired group. For some reason, negative energy always appears more powerful than the equivalent amount of positive influence. For this reason, the staff or group riding the horses of resistance need to be dealt with quickly and effectively.

An advantage of flat organizations is that they require few steps to get a decision made, and thus complete a project. By looking at your organization, you might discover that extra layers have crept into your company without your having realized it. The goal is to facilitate decision making, and if you discover that multiple levels of people must sign off and approve certain actions, you need to reevaluate your original goals.

If the Process Is Broken, Replace It

A well-run sourcing organization will have a staff able to make capable, well-researched recommendations for cost reductions and strategic improvements. A well-run company will have the process in place to quickly review the recommendation and ask for a minimum of additional information (and only that strictly required to make an informed decision). There is no room in this kind of organization for personnel who request obscure data having little to do with the project at hand.

Another difficult area to accept is the idea of a cost saving being ignored, a significant process improvement being abandoned, all because some computer-based data management system won't accommodate the recommendation.

Why would it ever be acceptable to ignore significantly improved efficiencies or cost-saving dollars because a system won't allow it? How could a conscientious, competitive manager of the new millennium not hear this and burst out laughing or crying, depending upon the severity, commitment, and depth of entrenchment of the impediment?

Systems are there as a tool, an aid toward making business more efficient and productive. They are designed to replace grunt work, simple calculations, and data accumulation tasks with a binary series of electrical impulses. Nothing more, nothing less. When the system becomes an impediment to continued success and growth, the twenty-first-century manager should not think twice about ripping it out and starting over again.

Empowering Your People

A smart organization will hire and promote personnel above the level of capability and performance required at the moment. A key to continued success is to have the staff in place ahead of the growth curve. Don't wait to hire them as current demand outstrips current capability. Hire people with the expectation that, as the company grows, the job will grow to match the skill levels of the people already in place.

Once these people are on board, train them well. Teach them the intricacies of the company, markets, product strengths, and weaknesses. Open your kimono to show the skeleton upon which the future successes will be built. Look into your company training culture for opportunities to excel. Sourcing is a job that people are trained to grow into, and although there are many fine degreed programs available and more coming on line every day, don't wait for the graduates to knock on your door. Create your own university of achievement.

Mentoring is an old technique, but one that continues to be very successful when correctly managed. Look to the bright stars of your current staff, and assign them responsibility for mentoring new people. Create a program that encourages a free exchange of ideas and suggestions; make sure there is time for regular meetings and conversations in everyone's schedules. Make the program a part of the mentor's regular progress review.

Drive your mentored employees with higher levels of responsibility. Their success and future will be tied, in part, to the results gained through the mentoring program. Encourage them to ask questions, to share projects, to not be afraid to change directions when there are changes in the business or markets. They must be held accountable for their personal success by identifying their needs and obtaining results from the mentoring program.

Encourage your staff to enroll in off-site training programs and courses. There are countless one- to three-day programs offered daily around the country. Make it a measurement of progress for each staff member to take such a course at least once or twice a year. They are investing in your success, but also in their own careers. No matter the cost, or who spends the dollars, it is an investment in everyone's future.

Look into professional affiliations, subscribe to journals, and read the constantly changing literature covering all aspects of the sourcing arena. The goal is a skillful, well-trained, sourcing department just itching to tackle the problems about to face them.

Knowing When to Get Out of the Way

Once they are trained and in place, the twenty-first-century manager will get out of her staff's way. She will know how and when to let them do the job they were hired to do.

The successful manager will encourage creative thought and innovation. She will be generous with praise and support, encouraging staff to make decisions on their own, offering the opportunity to bask in success, and to learn from failure. She will be stingy and Scrooge-like with criticism, finding an opportunity to learn and teach from missteps instead of taking them as a measure of personal weakness or failure. She will strongly believe in this concept: "My team gets all the credit for successes. I own all missteps."

The successful manager will not burden her staff with a blizzard of report and status requests, endless briefing meetings, and constant checking and double-checking of their work. She confidently assumes progress is on schedule, tasks and goals are being met, and potential or real problems are being handled correctly and efficiently. Once the team has come to terms on a project or task, unless told specifically otherwise by the team member himself, she confidently assumes that everything is on schedule and going according to plan. That is empowerment.

Summary

A key to being a wise, effective, and efficient manager is to hire the strongest staff possible. This manager will have a team of creative, independent sourcing specialists, people who take pride in addressing a problem and coming up with a solution. They will be a group that enjoys the challenge and personal recognition of a job well done. What they are not is needy.

Outstanding sourcing specialists do not need a manager constantly second-guessing their decisions, spending the day looking over their shoulder, or constantly requesting status updates. A weak manager will be quickly found out, and his fears and insecurities will filter out, encouraging talented personnel to look elsewhere for opportunities to exercise their skills.

This book talks a great deal about the role of the sourcing specialist. This chapter focuses on the changing management role, and what is required of the manager of the new sourcing team.

Management's role is to provide general guidance, support, training, and performance reinforcement to the people. It is responsible for providing the required work environment for its staff to work effectively. This century's manager is a cheerleader for success, a sounding board for questions and doubts, willing to shoulder responsibility for failure.

What's the key ingredient for success in managing the sourcing department of the future? It is to hire people with skill sets above your current needs. The job will catch up. Train your people often and well. Offer a strong support network that encourages creative solutions, including lauding the failures. The failures open the avenue of success. Finally, get out of your staff's way. Free them from wasted meetings and redundant reports, and encourage them to pursue activities that yield profitable results.

Epilogue

IN THIS CENTURY sourcing will be right in the heart of the new way of conducting business, and it will be an exciting and innovative department to be a part of.

I have tried to share that sense of excitement in each chapter of this book. Over the course of the twenty-three chapters, I have tried to expose you to the many changing facets and new ways of thinking "success" in the future. This book is a stepping-stone along the path of an important career, one with a real opportunity to make a difference. Good luck on your journey.

References

BELOW IS A LISTING of suggested companies and Web sites for further information on some of the topics introduced in this book. This is not intended to be a complete or comprehensive list. Rather, it is more of a starting point for your own research.

Product and Financial References

Dun & Bradstreet
Information Service Payment Report
Supplier Evaluation Report
Business Information Report
One Diamond Hill Road
Murray Hill, NJ 07974-1218
800-879-1362
www.dnb.com

Thomas Register
(twenty-three-book set or CD-ROM)
800-699-9822
www.ThomasRegister.com

Employee and Company Training

Chester Karrass
8370 Wilshire Boulevard
Beverly Hills, CA 90211-2333
323-951-7500
www.karrass.com

Oliver Wight Americas
12 Newport Road
New London, NH 03257
800-258-3862
www.ollie.com

Padgett-Thompson
Division of American Management Association
11221 Roe Avenue
Leawood, KS 66211
800-356-5107
913-491-2619
913-451-2109 (fax)

Saddle Island Institute
126 State Street
Boston, MA 02109
617-720-9545
617-720-9507 (fax)
www.saddleisland.com

Professional Associations and Trade Magazines

American Purchasing Society
North Island Center
8 East Galena Boulevard
Suite 203
Aurora, IL 60506
630-859-0250
630-859-0270 (fax)
www.american-purchasing.com
Two certification programs are offered: certified purchasing professional (CPP) and certified professional purchasing manager (CPPM).

Caucus
Association of High-Tech Procurement Professionals
Drawer 2970
Winter Park, FL 32790-2970
407-740-5600
407-740-0368 (fax)
E-mail: Info@caucusnet.com
www.caucusnet.com

The Educational Society for Resource Management
(formerly American Production & Inventory Control Society)
5301 Shawnee Road
Alexandria, VA 22312
800-444-2742
www.apics.org

Institute for Supply Management
2055 E. Centennial Circle
Tempe, AZ 85285-2160
800-888-6276
www.ism.ws
www.napm.org

National Association of Purchasing Card Professionals
P.O. Box 184
Excelsior, MN 55331
763-208-4914
www.napcp.org

National Association of State Procurement Professionals
167 West Main Street
Suite 600
Lexington, KY 40507
859-514-9159
www.naspo.org

National Institute of Governmental Purchasing
(professional government purchasing agent association)
151 Spring Street
Herndon, VA 20170-5223
800-367-6447
www.nigp.org

Outsourcing Institute
(neutral outsourcing professional association)
Jericho Atrium
500 N. Broadway
Suite 141
Jericho, NY 11753
516-681-0066
516-938-1839 (fax)
www.outsourcing.com

Purchasing Magazine
275 Washington Street
Newton, MA 02458
617-964-3030
www.manufacturing.net/pur/

Outsourcing Companies, Programs, and Software

Ariba
807 11th Avenue
Sunnyvale, CA 94089
650-390-1000
www.ariba.com

B2eMarkets
3202 Tower Oaks Boulevard
Rockville, MD 20852
877-405-6103
301-230-2248 (fax)
www.b2emarkets.com

Clarus
3970 Johns Creek Court
Suwanee, GA 30024
800-437-0734
770-291-8599 (fax)
www.claruscorp.com

eBreviate
2125 Oak Grove Road
Suite 200

Walnut Creek, CA 94598
888-327-3842
925-287-6301 (fax)
www.ebreviate.com

FreeMarkets, Inc.
(auction site/sourcing software)
210 Sixth Avenue
Pittsburgh, PA 15222
888-434-0500
www.freemarkets.com

Frictionless Commerce, Inc.
400 Technology Square
Floor 9
Cambridge, MA 02139
617-495-0180
617-495-0188 (fax)
www.frictionless.com

Frontstep Inc.
2800 Corporate Exchange Drive
Columbus, OH 43231
614-523-7000
614-895-2504 (fax)
www.frontstep.com

Global Exchange Services
(transaction outsourcing)
Division of G.E.
100 Edison Park Drive
Gaithersburg, MD 20878
800-560-4347
www.gxs.com

i2 Technology
One i2 Place
11701 Luna Road
Dallas, TX 75234
800-800-3288
214-860-6060 (fax)
www.i2technologies.com

J.D. Edwards
One Technology Way
Denver, CO 80237
877-613-9412
www.jdedwards.com

MindFlow
6504 International Parkway
Suite 2400
Plano, TX 75093
972-930-9988
www.mindflow.com

Oracle Systems
500 Oracle Parkway
Redwood City, CA 94065-1677
650-506-0794
www.oracle.com

Perfect Commerce Inc.
1860 Embarcadero Road
Suite 210
Palo Alto, CA 94303-3320
650-798-3335
650-858-1095 (fax)
www.perfect.com

Supply Works
34 Crosby Drive
Bedford, MA 01730
781-301-7000
781-301-7010 (fax)
www.supplyworks.com

Verticalnet
300 Chester Field Parkway
Malvern, PA 19355
610-240-0600
610-240-9470 (fax)
www.verticalnet.com

XPORTA
275 Saratoga Avenue

Suite 260
Santa Clara, CA 95050
866-490-0853
866-556-1401 (fax)
www.exporta.com

Quality Standards and Associations

American Society of Quality (ASQ)
600 North Plankinton Avenue
Milwaukee, WI 53203
800-248-1946
414-272-1734 (fax)
www.asq.org

The Association for Quality and Participation
(formerly International Association of Quality Circles)
P.O. Box 2055
Milwaukee, WI 53201-2055
800-513-381-0700 (fax)
www.aqp.org

Baldrige Quality Award
National Institute of Standards and Technology
Technology Administration
U.S. Department of Commerce
100 Bureau Drive
Gaithersburg, MD 20899-1020
301-975-2036
www.quality.nist.gov

International Organization for Standardization (ISO)
(ISO information and standards for ISO 9000)
www.iso.org

National Institute of Standards and Technology
U.S. Department of Commerce
100 Bureau Drive
Gaithersburg, MD 20899-3460
301-975-6478
www.nist.gov

Juran Institute, Inc.
115 Old Ridgefield Road
Wilton, CT 06897
203-834-1700
www.Juran.com

The W. Edwards Deming Institute
P.O. Box 59511
Potomac, MD 20859-9511
301-294-8405
301-294-8406 (fax)
www.deming.org

Search Engines

Google
www.google.com

Lycos
www.lycos.com

MSN
www.msn.com

Yahoo
www.yahoo.com

Netscape
www.netscape.com

Prokudos
www.prokudos.com
(purchasing, materials management search site)

Suggested Reading

BELOW IS A LIST of some of the latest books that relate to modern sourcing. They are loosely grouped by into six classifications: e-commerce, global, law, negotiation, quality, and strategy.

E-Commerce

Neef, Dale. *E-Procurement: From Strategy to Implementation*. London: Financial Times/Prentice Hall, 2001.

Global

Ashley, James M. *International Purchasing Handbook*. Upper Saddle River, N.J.: Prentice-Hall, Inc., 1997.

Fcit, Alan E. and Alan Branch. *International Purchasing and Management*. London: International Thomson Business Press, 2001.

Krotseng, Lee. *Global Sourcing*. West Palm Beach, Fla.: PT Publications, 1997.

Law

Badenhoff, William F., John P Mahoney, and Mark M. Grieco. *Purchasing Contract Law, UCC & Patents*. West Palm Beach, Fla.: PT Publications, 1998.

Grieco, Jr., Peter L., and William F. Badenhoff. *Purchasing Ethics*. West Palm Beach, Fla.: PT Publications, 1998.

King, Donald Barnett, and James J. Ritterskamp. *Purchasing Manager's Desk Book of Purchasing Law*. Upper Saddle River, N.J.: Prentice Hall Trade, 1998.

Negotiation

Aherman, Sandy, Ira G. Asherman. *25 Role Plays for Negotiation Skills*. Amherst, Mass.: HRD Press, 1997.

Acuff, Frank L. *How to Negotiate Anything with Anyone, Anywhere Around the World*. New York: AMACOM, 1997.

Brett, Jeanne M. *Negotiate Globally: How to Negotiate Deals, Resolve Disputes, and Make Decisions Across Cultures*. San Francisco: Jossey-Bass, 2001.

Dawson, Roger. *Secrets of Power Negotiating: Inside Secrets from a Master Negotiator*. Franklin Lakes, N.J.: Career Press, 1999.

Karrass, Chester L. *Give and Take: The Complete Guide to Negotiating Strategies and Tactics*. New York: Harper Business, 1995.

Karrass, Chester L. *In Business as in Life, You Don't Get What You Deserve, You Get What You Negotiate*. Santa Monica, Calif.: Stanford Street Press, 1996.

Kramer, Henry S. *Game, Set, Match: Winning the Negotiations Game*. New York: ALM Publishing, 2001.

Saunders, David M., Bruce Barry, Roy J. Lewicki, and John W. Minton. *Negotiation: Readings, Exercises, and Cases*. New York: Irwin/McGraw-Hill, 2002.

Shapiro, Ronald M., Mark A. Jankowski, James Dale, and Cal Ripkin. *The Power of Nice: How to Negotiate So Everyone Wins—Especially You*. New York: John Wiley & Sons, 2001.

Thompson, Leigh L. *The Mind and Heart of the Negotiator*. Saddle River, N.J.: Prentice-Hall, 2000.

Tipler, Julia. *Successful Negotiating*. New York: AMACOM, 2000.

Volkema, Roger J. *The Negotiation Toolkit: How to Get Exactly What You Want in Any Business or Personal Situation*. New York: AMACOM, 1999.

Zick, Bernard. *The Negotiating Paradox: How You Can Get More by Giving More.* Dallas: Skyward Publishing Co., 1999.

Strategy

Ayers, James B. *Handbook of Supply Chain Management.* Jamaica Hills, N.Y.: Saint Lucie Press, 2000.

Baily, Peter. *Purchasing Principles and Management.* Upper Saddle River, N.J.: Financial Times/Prentice-Hall, 1998.

Banfield, Emiko. *Harness Value in the Supply Chain: Strategic Sourcing in Action.* New York: John Wiley & Sons, Inc., 1999.

Boone, Tonya and Ram Ganeshan. *New Directions in Supply-Chain Management: Technology, Strategy, and Implementation.* New York: AMACOM, 2002.

Burt, David N., and Richard L. Pinkerton. *A Purchasing Manager's Guide to Strategic Proactive Procurement.* New York: AMACOM, 1995.

Carliss, Baldwin, and Joan Magretta. *Harvard Business Review on Managing the Value Chain.* Boston: Harvard Business School Press, 2000.

Carter, Stephen. *Successful Purchasing.* Haupauge, N.Y.: Barron's Education Series, 1997.

Cavinato, Joseph L., and Ralph G. Kauffman. *The Purchasing Handbook: A Guide for the Purchasing and Supply Professional.* New York: McGraw-Hill Professional Publishing, 1999.

Dale, Barrie, and Bernard Burnes. *Working in Partnership: Best Practice in Customer-Supplier Relations.* Hampshire, England: Gower Publishing, Co., 1998.

Domberger, Simon. *The Contracting Organization: A Strategic Guide to Outsourcing.* New York: Oxford University Press, 1999.

Erridge, Andrew, Ruth Fee, and John McIlroy. *Best Practice Procurement: Public and Private Sector Perspectives.* Hampshire, England: Gower Publishing Co., 2001.

Gay, Charles L., and James Essinger. *Inside Outsourcing.* London: Nicholas Brealey, 2000.

Goldfield, Charles. *Supplier Strategies*. West Palm Beach, Fla.: PT Publications, 1999.

Greaver, Maurice F. *Strategic Outsourcing: A Structured Approach to Outsourcing Decision and Initiatives*. New York: AMACOM, 1998.

Greico, Peter L. *MRO Purchasing*. West Palm Beach, Fla.: PT Publications, 1997.

Grieco, Peter L., and Carl R. Cooper. *Power Purchasing: Supply Management in the 21st Century*. West Palm Beach, Fla.: PT Publications, 1995.

Halvey, John K., and Barbara Murphy Melby. *Business Process Outsourcing: Process, Strategies, and Contracts*. New York: John Wiley & Sons, Inc., 1999.

Harding, Michael, and Mary Lu Harding. *Purchasing*. Haupauge, N.Y.: Barron's Educational Series, 2001.

Hough, Harry. *Purchasing for Manufacturing*. New York: Industrial Press, 1996.

Hough, Harry. *Purchasing Fundamentals for Today's Buyer*. Saddle River, N.J.: Prentice-Hall, Inc.,1998.

Johnson, Mike. *Outsourcing: In Brief*. Woburn, Mass.: Butterworth-Heinemann, 1997.

Kuglin, Fred A. *Customer-Centered Supply Chain Management: A Link-by-Link Guide*. New York: AMACOM, 1998.

Laseter, Timothy M. *Balanced Sourcing: Cooperation and Competition in Supplier Relationships*. San Francisco: Jossey-Bass, 1998.

Leenders, Michael R., Harold E. Fearon, Anna E. Flynn, and P. Fraser Johnson. *Purchasing and Supply Management*. New York: McGraw Hill Higher Education, 2001.

Leenders, Michael R., and Anna E. Flynn. *Value Driven Purchasing: Managing the Key Steps in the Acquisition Process*. New York: McGraw-Hill Professional Publishing, 1994.

Lewis, Jordan D. *The Connected Corporation: How Leading Companies Win Through Customer-Supplier Alliances*. New York: Free Press, 1995.

Mahoney, P., Linda S. Keckler, and Ben Laaper. *Procurement Reengineering*. West Palm Beach, Fla.: PT Publications, 1998.

Maromonte, Kevin R. *Corporate Strategic Business Sourcing*. Westport, Conn.: Greenwood Publishing Group, Inc., 1998.

Mentzer, John T. *Supply Chain Management*. Thousand Oaks, Calif.: Sage Publications, Inc., 2001.

Moore, Randy A. *The Science of High-Performance Supplier Management*. New York: AMACOM, 2001.

Morgan, James P. *Plain Talk About Purchasing*. Newton, Mass.: Reed Business Information, 2000.

Nellore, Rajesh, and Samuel M. Hines, Jr. *Managing Buyer-Supplier Relations: The Winning Edge Through Specification Management*. New York: Routledge, 2001.

Nelson, Dave, Particia E. Moody, and John Stegner. *The Purchasing Machine: How Top Ten Companies Use Best Practices to Manage Their Supply Chains*. New York: Free Press, 2001.

Nichols, Jr., Ernest, and Robert B. Hansfield. *Supply Chain Redesign: Transforming Supply Chains into Integrated Value Systems*. London: Financial Times Management, 2002.

Riggs, David A. and Sharon L. Robbins. *The Executive's Guide to Supply Management Strategies: Building Supply Chain Thinking into All Business Processes*. New York: AMACOM, 1998.

Rudman, Jack. *Principal Purchasing Agent*. Syosset, N.Y.: National Learning Corp., 2000.

Saunders, Malcolm J. *Strategic Purchasing and Supply Chain Management*. Philadelphia: Trans-Atlantic Publications, 2000.

Scheuing, Eberhard E., and Bill Christopher. *Value-Added Purchasing: Partnering for World-Class Performance*. Menlo Park, Calif.: Crisp Publications, Inc., 1998.

Schorr, John E. *Purchasing in the 21st Century: A Guide to State-of-the-Art Techniques and Strategies*. New York: John Wiley & Sons, Inc., 1998.

van Weele, Arjan. *Purchasing and Supply Chain Management: Analysis, Planning, and Practice*. London: International Thomson Business Press, 2001.

Wood, John A., and NAPM staff. *Purchasing and Supply Yearbook: The 2000 Edition*. New York: McGraw-Hill Education Group, 1999.

Quality

Bhote, Keki R., and Adi K. Bhote. *World Class Quality, 2nd Edition: Using Design of Experiments to Make it Happen*. New York: AMACOM, 1999.

Fernandez, Ricardo R. *Total Quality in Purchasing and Supplier Management*. Jamaica Hills, N.Y.: St. Lucie Press, 1994.

Kaynak, Hale. *Total Quality Management and Just-in-Time Purchasing: Their Effects on Performance of Firms Operating in the U.S.* New York: Garland Publishing, Inc., 1997.

Index

ten-minute-more analysis, 6,
137–138
tickets and professional-level ethics,
178, 179
trademark laws and Chinese business relations, 166
Traficant, James, and professional-level ethics, 175–176
training, employee and company,
164, 171, 190–191, 196
trucking companies (local) and vendor consolidation, 35

Universal Commercial Code
(U.C.C.), 136

vendor-managed inventory
Kan Ban manual ordering system,
89
paperwork, cutting back on,
57–58

smaller companies competing
with largest ones, 105
technology, harnessing the tools
of, 97
see also certification, vendor; consolidation, vendor; management, vendor; performance,
vendor
vertical integration as standard in
the past, 75

wait time and lead time, 118
win-win negotiations, 10, 141–142
working conditions and Chinese
business relations, 166
WorldCom, 175

Xerox, 162, 175

Yahoo!, 94